# 50 Situations

## Awaiting Every Forensic Scientist

# 50 Situations

## Awaiting Every Forensic Scientist

A Professional Effectiveness Handbook

JOHN M. COLLINS

Critical Victories, LLC
901 S. Bridge Street
P.O. Box 227
Dewitt, MI 48820

**www.criticalvictories.com**
(51) 803-4063

Copyright © 2020 by Critical Victories, LLC

All rights reserved. No part of this publication may be reproduced, distributed, or transmitted in any form or by any means, including photocopying, recording, or other electronic or mechanical methods, without the prior written permission of the publisher, except in the case of brief quotations embodied in critical reviews and certain other noncommercial uses permitted by copyright law.

For permission requests, contact Critical Victories, LLC at office@criticalvictories.com or at www.criticalvictories.com.

The author of this book is available for speaking engagements, and public appearances. Please contact the author for information at office@criticalvictories.com or at (517) 803-4063.

Manufactured in the United States of America.

ISBN: 978-1-09835-111-3
ISBN: 978-1-09835-112-0 (ebook)

Author:   John M. Collins MA, SHRM-SCP

To My Parents, John and Sharon

We Miss You

# Contents

Other Books by the Author
Author's Note

Introduction................................................................1

## Part 1 – Your Employment

| | | |
|---|---|---|
| 1 | First Day of Work............................................. | 13 |
| 2 | Scientific Training............................................ | 15 |
| 3 | Casework Authorization.................................. | 17 |
| 4 | Imperfect Laboratory...................................... | 19 |
| 5 | Career Doubt................................................... | 21 |
| 6 | Case Backlogs.................................................. | 27 |
| 7 | Excessive Focus on Productivity..................... | 29 |
| 8 | Excessive Focus on Quality............................. | 31 |
| 9 | Change.............................................................. | 33 |
| 10 | Conflict............................................................ | 35 |
| 11 | Boredom........................................................... | 39 |
| 12 | Collateral Assignments................................... | 41 |
| 13 | Making a Recommendation............................. | 43 |
| 14 | Giving a Speech or Presentation..................... | 48 |
| 15 | Feeling Stuck in Your Position........................ | 51 |
| 16 | Compensation Frustration............................... | 53 |
| 17 | Being a Partner to Management...................... | 57 |
| 18 | Supporting your Parent Agency....................... | 59 |
| 19 | Civilian Discrimination................................... | 61 |
| 20 | Workplace Injury............................................. | 63 |

## Part 2 – Your Professionalism and Integrity

| | | |
|---|---|---|
| 21 | Accreditation Assessments.............................. | 67 |
| 22 | Attendance at Professional Conferences......... | 69 |
| 23 | Disagreeing with the Conclusion of a Peer..... | 71 |

| 24 | Disagreeing with the Conclusion of a Supervisor....... 73 |
|---|---|
| 25 | Being Tempted to Lie or Cheat............................. 75 |
| 26 | Confronting Misconduct in the Laboratory.............. 77 |
| 27 | Harassment by Review........................................ 79 |
| 28 | Making an Error................................................. 81 |
| 29 | Loss of Self-Confidence...................................... 83 |

## Part 3 - Expert Witnessing

| 30 | Courtroom Anxiety............................................. 89 |
|---|---|
| 31 | Defending Your Science...................................... 91 |
| 32 | Silenced in the Courtroom.................................... 95 |
| 33 | Conclusion Dismissed as *Just* Your Opinion........... 97 |
| 34 | Answering Leading Questions............................... 99 |
| 35 | Courtroom Admonishment................................... 101 |
| 36 | Prosecutorial Bias............................................... 103 |
| 37 | Sympathy for the Defendant................................. 105 |
| 38 | Expressing Your Scientific Certainty..................... 107 |
| 39 | Feeling Joy or Sadness About a Verdict................. 109 |
| 40 | Distrusted Due to Police Affiliations..................... 111 |
| 41 | Believing Strongly that the Defendant is Guilty........ 113 |
| 42 | Believing Strongly that the Defendant is Innocent..... 115 |
| 43 | Helping Out the Court Reporter............................ 117 |
| 44 | Court Orders and Judicial Pressures...................... 119 |
| 45 | Cynicism........................................................... 121 |

## Part 4 - Thinking About Your Future

| 46 | Considering a Management Position..................... 125 |
|---|---|
| 47 | Becoming a First-Time Manager.......................... 127 |
| 48 | Enjoying Your Career......................................... 129 |
| 49 | Uplifting Your Coworkers................................... 133 |
| 50 | Being a Forensic Science Ambassador.................. 135 |

Conclusion............................................................... 137
Appendix.................................................................. 143
About the Author....................................................... 195

# Other Books by the Author

**HR Management in the Forensic Science Laboratory**
*A 21$^{st}$ Century Approach to Effective Crime Lab Leadership*

Published by Academic Press, 2018

**Crime Lab Report**
*An Anthology on Forensic Science in the Era of Criminal Justice Reform*

Published by Academic Press, 2019

# 50 Situations
Awaiting Every Forensic Scientist

## Author's Note

Given the intense adversarial nature of the American criminal justice system, I suspect this book could be used as a tool to impeach practicing forensic scientists or to otherwise discredit their work and laboratories. Excerpts of this book might even be read in open court as a way to either challenge or reinforce the credentials of expert witnesses. I wish to make clear that this book was not written for such a purpose. It was not written to be tendered as evidence and I strongly discourage it from being used as such. This book was written solely for the professional development of forensic laboratory scientists.

I'd also like to remind readers that any advice or recommendations I make in this book are strictly my opinions and are based on my own professional experience as a forensic scientist, forensic science administrator, executive coach, and instructor. Like me, you are responsible for the outcomes resulting from your words and conduct, including any actions you take based on what you learn in this book. In *everything* you do, please be competent, professional, ethical, and moral.

# INTRODUCTION

Great careers happen on purpose, not by accident

The vast majority of forensic scientists working today, in my opinion, are living out careers that differ sharply from what they first expected. I include myself in this company because I never could have imagined in a million years how my career would unfold. As a young college student learning under the tutelage of Dr. Jay Siegel at Michigan State University, it would have been impossible for me to anticipate the opportunities I would have, the challenges I would confront, the crimes I would investigate, the evidence I would analyze, the people I would meet, the situations I would encounter, and the twists and turns my career would take when I least expected them.

If it hasn't already, your career will take its share of twists and turns too. Who you become as a forensic science professional will result from the accumulation of experiences, both expected and unexpected, that will weave themselves into a tapestry of knowledge, skills, insights, opinions, sentiments, thoughts, ideas, and emotions. At any one moment, you may find yourself reflecting back on your career and realizing that your body of expertise is entirely and completely unique. No other human being on the planet will have amassed the exact same compilation of professional memories as you. Every day that you continue to work as a forensic scientist will strengthen, deepen, and broaden your expertise. You will find, as I did, that the uniqueness of your expertise will often manifest itself subtly in the resulting uniqueness of the opportunities and challenges you encounter along the way. These opportunities and challenges will require you to make decisions, and those decisions will influence how your career unfolds.

Forensic science is not as easy as outsiders find it interesting. There are occupational dynamics inherent to the experience of working in forensic science that require mental, emotional, and even physical stamina. Obvious to most people is the emotional strain of witnessing the horrors of violent crime. Some forensic scientists are confronted with this more than others, especially those who visit crime scenes or observe autopsies. For other forensic scientists, the experience of testifying as an expert witness in a court of law is especially unnerving. Yet, in my experience, these do not represent the most difficult parts of working in forensic science.

For me and for many others with whom I've discussed the challenges of working in forensic science, perhaps the most frustrating is working within a criminal justice system that, at times, seems to make absolutely no sense. It is adversarial, turbulent, reactive, cynical, inefficient, highly political, and populated with some gruff personalities and insatiable egos who sometimes seem to go out of their way to be as unpleasant as possible. And for the civilian / non-sworn forensic scientists working in police agencies, reporting to police commanders having little experience or interest in science requires an almost superhuman degree of personal patience and diplomacy.

But for all of the frustrations one will encounter in a forensic science career, in a strange way they are also what make it so rewarding – if you are willing to accept the challenge. As forensic scientists, we are graced with the honor and privilege of being beacons of light within a raging storm. Within a powerful institution dominated by cops, lawyers, judges, and jurors, we get to be *scientists* – politely insistent on meeting our responsibilities to give a voice to physical evidence that cannot speak for itself. We are translators, of sorts, helping criminal justice authorities understand the hidden messages that only scientific methods can decipher.

The key, therefore, to enjoying a meaningful and satisfying career in forensic science is embracing the chaos and putting it in its proper place. This chaos should not impair you. It is nothing more than a playing field, something you mustn't take personally or be troubled by. It is what it is and there is nothing that you nor I can do to change it. Just as football players play on a football field, basketball players play on a basketball court, and hockey players play on an ice rink, forensic scientists *play* in the rough and tumble of the criminal justice system.

If you are inclined to think this chaos is singularly challenging for forensic scientists, it is even harder on the leaders and administrators in charge of forensic science laboratories. At the outset, I wish to encourage you to be empathetic and supportive of your laboratory administrators as they attempt to negotiate the political, economic, and legal nuances of contemporary criminal justice. One day it may be *you* in charge, and you will expect the same courtesy.

There is a lot about criminal justice that is broken, about which I wrote extensively in *Crime Lab Report*. The good news, however, is that it is slowly changing for the better. It is my opinion that the growing dependence of police, prosecutors, defenders, and judges on scientific evidence is among the many forces that are driving positive change. Criminal justice is becoming increasingly professional. So, the best thing you can do is *be* a professional, be competent, and be as ethical as possible in everything you do and in every situation you encounter. The rest will take care of itself in good time.

This means, of course, that you should expect your career to place you in a variety of situations that will require you to make choices. The quality of the choices you make will predict the quality of the outcomes you experience. Some of these choices will be very specific, such as what method to employ in the analysis of an unusual piece of evidence. They may also be broad and professionally significant, such as the decision to engage in secondary employment as a faculty adjunct at a local community college. Everything about your career and the value you derive from that career will arise from the choices you make.

This begs a reasonable question: What are some of the most impactful but common situations in which forensic scientists may find themselves having to make difficult choices? Can we predict what these situations might be so that you can be better prepared, enhancing your chances of making the right choices when circumstances require them? The answer is an emphatic yes, and they are why this book was written.

I began my career in forensic science as an unpaid college intern at the Michigan State Police forensic science laboratory in Sterling Heights, Michigan – about 20 miles north of Detroit. Earning 12 college credits and no money for my labors, I was assigned to the latent fingerprint unit where I conducted research on how fluorescing dye stains performed on different substrates when used to detect latent fingerprints. It was during the summer of 1992, a time during which communities in the metro Detroit area were on the lookout for a man believed to have murdered multiple prostitutes, leaving their bodies to decompose in the hot summer sun. During the autopsy of one victim, the medical examiner severed both hands from the body so they could be sent to our laboratory in Sterling Heights. The advanced decomposition and wrinkling of the skin negated the possibility that an ink-rolled fingerprint could be collected at the morgue, entered into the database of the Automated Fingerprint Identification System (AFIS), and possibly allow for the identity of the victim to be determined.

When the hands arrived at our lab, the fingers were curled, making it impossible to attempt an ink roll. The scientists assigned to the case decided that a pair of cutters – the kind you would buy at a hardware store – should be used to cut off the fingers. They did not cut through bone so easily so they called for me, a bulky and recently retired discus thrower from Michigan State University, to muscle the cutter blades through the bone so that the fingers could be processed further.

At this point in my life, the task I was asked to perform was officially the most disgusting thing I had ever done. The hands were infested with maggots, which caused the hands to shake and twitch as if they were alive.

The sound of the cutters breaking through the bone made a sound similar to that heard when breaking a tree branch in half. After the fingers were removed, the skin of each fingertip was easily slipped *off* the finger and slipped *onto* the gloved hand of a scientist who rolled a perfect fingerprint, which eventually led to the identification of the victim and the subsequent arrest of the perpetrator. All of this happened within the first few days of my internship, something I will never forget.

Although I didn't know it at the time, this experience was a harbinger of the kinds of strange and memorable experiences I would have throughout my career. It is not my intention here to be autobiographical, so I won't. But I do wish to emphasize how your career in forensic science, as mine was, will be defined by the moments and situations that come and go with the passage of time. As a friend and colleague of mine once observed, "my memories are like a slide show that play in my head." Indeed, it is this way for me. Some of those slides are pleasant; some are disturbing. But they all comprise the totality of my professional being, as they will for you. That day when I was cutting off the fingers of a serial killer's victim, I could not have predicted that one day I would become the director of forensic science for the state of Michigan and therefore responsible for the operations of the Sterling Heights laboratory, as well as the other six laboratories operated in Michigan. That such an awesome opportunity eventually came to me was the result of things both in and out of my control. Choices I made in my life and in my career allowed me to *earn* such a prestigious position, but they just as easily could have prevented it.

In August of 2012, I made the difficult decision to retire my career as a forensic laboratory administrator, wanting to explore life in the private sector and eventually start my own private consulting practice. By then, I had earned my master's degree in organizational management and my professional HR certification through the Society for Human Resource Management, later becoming trained as an executive coach. Why did I choose to amass a set of credentials that have so little to do with forensic science? Because they have *everything* to do with forensic science; and they have everything to do with *you*. Let me take a moment to explain.

By the time I began my career in the early 1990s, the forensic laboratory sciences had made impressive strides in the areas of technology and quality assurance. DNA profiling, for example, was just coming online. Forensic laboratory accreditation was changing how scientists subjected their work, policies, and procedures to external scrutiny. Elaborate windows-based information-management systems were replacing paper logbooks and sluggish, homegrown mainframe systems, allowing casework data to be digitally archived, retrieved, and reported on a moment's notice. The 1990s were an interesting time to be a forensic scientist because so much was changing right before our eyes.

Not yet receiving serious attention, however, was the critical need to prioritize the improvement of leadership methods in forensic science laboratories. Of particular concern to me, the son of an HR director at an architectural firm near Detroit, was how poorly human-resource management practices were administered in forensic science laboratories. Because most laboratories were arranged as parts of law enforcement agencies (and they still are as of the writing of this book), the rapid evolution of forensic science was not being met with an equally rapid evolution of the leadership and managerial techniques employed in crime laboratories. As a result, many forensic science laboratories in the 1990s were rather unpleasant places to work, both physically and emotionally – and this certainly was the case for me.

The earliest years of my career were an exercise in emotional endurance. The laboratory where I started my career was infested with managers who were either abusive, incompetent, or both. I witnessed unacceptable demonstrations of racism, sexual hostility, and sexual harassment. It was widely suspected at the time that my supervisor was sleeping with one of my coworkers, and I remain convinced that it was true. This same coworker once accidentally discharged a 12-guage shotgun in the open laboratory, with the shot pellets traveling out the door, into the hallway, through a wall, and into an office whose occupant had stepped away for a few moments. His computer was in the path of the shot charge and was nearly destroyed.

I remember another troublesome day when I sat at my desk eating lunch while my supervisor and - you guessed it - my coworker had left town to attend a professional meeting together. From the corner of my eye, I noticed the assistant laboratory director (I'll call him Garrett), giving a tour to a distinguished looking man dressed in a sharp black suit – he looked like a federal agent. Garrett barked from the doorway leading into our unit, "Hey f*&% wad, where is your boss?" I could feel the blood rush to my face as I struggled to contain my anger, politely informing Garrett that my supervisor was out of town.

Many was the evening that I lay in bed wondering what I had gotten myself into – whether or not I wanted to continue in this field, and what I would do if I decided to get out. In my early 20s, I was demoralized, frustrated, and fearful of the future. With a bachelor's degree in forensic science, my options were limited. Over the next 17 years, I changed jobs, took promotions, and grew my career as would any ambitious professional struggling to find himself and his place in the world. But, in retrospect, I now see how the path of my career was leading me directly to a point where I would be uniquely suited to help improve the organizational cultures of forensic science laboratories throughout the United States and around the world. In doing so, perhaps I harbored a strong urge to ensure that as few forensic scientists as possible would ever have to endure what I did.

On this journey, I wrote two pioneering forensic science textbooks. The first was called *HR Management in the Forensic Science Laboratory – A 21st Century Approach to Effective Crime Lab Leadership*. The second was a book about criminal justice controversies and public policies related to forensic science called *Crime Lab Report*. Both books were published by Academic Press in 2018 and 2019 respectively, and because they are scholarly textbooks, they are rather expensive. So, for quite some time, I also envisioned writing a more personal book for forensic scientists about the sensitive situations in which they could reasonably expect to find themselves one day – any day - what they should be thinking about when they do, and what might happen if the right or wrong choices are made. Unlike my first two books, I also wanted this new book to be affordable to the average forensic scientist.

On the pages that follow, I present 50 specific professional situations for which I believe every forensic scientist should be prepared. Having experienced all of them, it is my hope that by helping you think about them now, you will be better positioned to deal with them effectively when you encounter them. Some of these situations occur in the lives of *every* forensic scientist; some, on the other hand, may *never* occur. Some are part of the natural course of a forensic science career; others are special situations that arise under special circumstances. It is my hope that this book creates opportunities for you as you expand your professional thinking and refine your understanding of what it means to be a professional. The best way to learn, of course, is by experiencing these situations in real life. But we can also learn great lessons by *anticipating* them, for it is in the anticipation of events that we marshal the mental, emotional, and physical resources needed to negotiate their complexities with greater ease and sophistication. Through anticipation, we experience that which has not yet happened.

As you continue on with your reading, I recognize that your career is unwinding like a river through the mountains. So is mine, even after all these years. There's turbulence and there's beauty. There's pleasantness and there's danger - but along the way, you will be strengthened by the power of *intention*. What I mean is that it's not necessary for you to be a spectator in your own life and in your own career, where the outcomes seem to happen by accident. You can, in fact, be a player empowered by the ability and opportunity to influence how your career plays out - but only if you accept the responsibilities that come with it. Your intentions and goodwill can survive anything your career may throw at you. But those intentions have to be clear to *you*, and you have to be committed to them. What are *you* committed to?

Forensic science is a rewarding and invigorating occupation that holds as many secrets as it does promises. Whatever you do, be conscious about taking time to reflect on the gratitude you have for being able to work in such a celebrated, respected field of endeavor. Millions of people around the world would love to have your job. Treat it with the respect it deserves as you treat yourself with the respect *you* deserve. And as you encounter some or all of the situations described in this book, and as you encounter any other situations that tax your mental and emotional energies, ask yourself this simple question:

*What would a world-class forensic scientist do in this situation?*

# PART 1

Your Employment

# 1

## First Day of Work

When you arrive for your first day of work at your new place of employment, you may quickly realize that the laboratory cannot shut itself down to give you the warmest of welcomes. Some laboratories are more advanced than others when it comes to onboarding new employees. Yours may have a well-designed, well-managed program aimed at maximizing the positive emotions you experience as you start your new job. If so, your first days of work will seem streamlined, organized, and intentional. This is as it should be because it will galvanize your sense of belonging to your new team and brighten the opinions you have of your laboratory and its administration.

If your first day of work, however, seems disorganized, disjointed, or a bit cold, don't take it personally. Remember that you are entering a technical and scientific environment where warmth and fuzziness are not necessarily key priorities. Just go with the flow and follow the instructions given to you. Ask questions if you feel lost or unsure of what to do. As you get a few more days and weeks behind you, you will begin to feel things lighten up as you meet more people and become more familiar with your new surroundings.

There are three key priorities to onboarding a new employee in a forensic science laboratory. The first is to teach you how to keep yourself safe. You will be introduced to your laboratory's health and safety controls and you will receive training on how to minimize your vulnerability to risk. The second is to keep you, the laboratory, your coworkers, and the evidence secure. You will likely be given keys and passcodes that allow you to pass through areas of the laboratory to which you are authorized access. Finally, the process of officially finalizing the details of your terms and conditions of employment will likely happen within the first two days of work. You will spend time with individuals responsible for the HR function of the laboratory who will have you complete standard forms and answer questions. This is all necessary to formally complete the process of employing you.

While all of this is happening, cases and evidence from crimes are flowing through the front door of the laboratory. Scientists are testifying in court and meeting with investigators. Laboratory administrators are negotiating with budget authorities on the purchase of new supplies and equipment. As a new employee, you are jumping onto a moving train, which can feel intimidating and humbling. But don't worry; it is likely that everyone else in the laboratory experienced the same feelings on their first days of work.

This is an exciting time that you mustn't allow to become unnecessarily soured by feelings of anxiousness or frustration. Simply observe what is happening around you and react accordingly. Soon, you will have a chance to tour the laboratory facility and meet many of its employees. Smile and allow yourself to be saturated with gratitude for the opportunity you have before you. Those you meet will sense your positivity and will be more likely to engage you in conversation. Although this first day of work will be a memory soon, it is an opportunity to begin your career with the right attitude.

# 2

## Scientific Training

It is the responsibility of your laboratory to present you to the criminal justice system as a reliable, trustworthy, and competent expert. This takes time and requires extensive training. The goal of your initial scientific training is not only to learn how to complete specific tasks in the laboratory but to also build a depth of knowledge and perspective that allows you to answer the kinds of questions that are likely to be asked by very experienced, clever trial attorneys whose goal it will be to weaken your credibility or the credibility of the testimony you give in court.

It is my hope and my expectation, however, that your professional curiosity will be bigger than the training program being administered to you. Yes, you have a program to complete and this program has been designed to give you the minimum competencies necessary to analyze evidence in actual criminal cases. But to be a true expert, you must be driven by curiosity and a sincere hunger to learn more. There is nothing your laboratory can do to unilaterally build your expertise and credibility. You must do this for yourself. Whenever possible, dive deeper into the topics and issues you study than what the training program is designed to cover. The effort you make will result in a body of knowledge and skill that will earn the confidence of the people with whom you interact, both inside and outside of the courtroom.

That being said, it's important that you follow your training program as it is designed to be followed and that you complete the work that is required. It is likely that you will encounter moments when you are confused or seem unable to grasp the concepts being taught. It is important that you press forward and have faith that you will come to understand that which you momentarily don't. This ongoing struggle to understand difficult concepts is as important as the lessons themselves. It forces you to actually *experience* the subject-matter and build your knowledge from within the depths of the material rather than from a superficial position of false knowing. The effort you make to struggle through the material is a clear sign of your commitment to the work and to the seriousness of the investment being made in you. True expertise is not easily attained, thank goodness.

One of the more frustrating things I've witnessed both in my career as a forensic scientist and as an executive coach are students more interested in putting on a show than actually learning. They have impressive educational credentials and want to be thought of as smart, capable, and without weakness, so they don't ask questions and refuse to admit when they are confused. This makes it utterly impossible for coaches or training managers to meet the needs of these grandstanders without some kind of corrective action or counseling. It is vital that you be honest with yourself and with those responsible for training you. If you insist on acting more knowledgeable and skilled than you actually are, you will raise serious questions about your integrity and honesty.

Your training is a time when you have permission to be confused and make mistakes with minimal consequence. Most new forensic scientists complete their training successfully. Those who don't are usually of sufficient intelligence and ability but are impaired by destructive attitudes about their own abilities and an inappropriate obsession about how they are perceived.

# 3

## Casework Authorization

Your scientific training concludes with what is known as a *competency test*, which can take a number of different forms depending on the goals of your laboratory and the structure of the training program. Once the laboratory confirms that you are *trained to competency*, you will be permitted to engage in actual casework with limited or no special supervision.

Casework authorization is an exciting and important moment in your career as a forensic scientist because it is the moment where you get to do what you were hired to do. Armed with so much knowledge and skill, you are undoubtedly itching to start using it in service of the cause of justice. You are now a fully trained and practicing forensic scientist!

Nothing needs to be said here to dull the enthusiasm you feel at this moment, but it is important to be mindful that there is much more learning to do and experiences to be had. Even though your *training* is complete, your *expertise* is remarkably narrow compared to what it will be 3 or 5 years from now. So, it behooves you to be humble about and respectful of both your capabilities and limitations.

The biggest risk you face right now is working at a speed and pace that your expertise cannot keep up with. Trust me, your laboratory leaders are as excited as you to have your training completed and they want you to start contributing to the overall production of the laboratory. There are cases to be worked and there is evidence to be tested. They invested in your training so that you could become part of the team responsible for getting the work done. But your confidence and enthusiasm must be tempered by an awareness that you have not yet mastered the skills needed to work quickly and reliably at the same time. For you, the threshold at which your hurriedness begins to threaten quality comes much sooner than those with more experience. This is certainly not to suggest that you should be slow or cumbersome in your work. Indeed, you should not because part of your competency is the ability to work reliably at a *reasonable* speed. But I do wish to encourage your exercise of caution and your willingness to double check your work so as to minimize the possibility for error.

Finally, the less-than-engaged forensic scientist may succumb to the temptation of believing that the time for learning has now come and gone. After all, you are working cases now, doing what you were hired to do. But for the *world-class* forensic scientist, the learning now begins. Even as you dive into the cases and evidence awaiting your attention, learning and improvement must be constant themes in your professional activities. It is up to you to ensure this happens. Genuine experts think of themselves as students first. They have such a strong curiosity about their subject-matter areas that they crave knowledge and work diligently to attain it. Over time, it expands into rich and valuable bodies of experiences and perspectives. Now that you are authorized to conduct casework, let this be the beginning of your learning, that moment in time when you begin to build the structure of credentials and qualifications that will define you as a professional in the years to come. The effort starts now. It is up to you and *only* you to make that happen.

# 4

## Imperfect Laboratory

Given enough time, every forensic scientist realizes that her laboratory is not perfect, that her managers don't know everything, and that some of her colleagues have personalities or quirks that are annoying or downright irritating. Her supervisor might be moody, the laboratory facilities might be less than modern, and some of her coworkers might be gossipers or complainers of Olympic proportion. The honeymoon is over, so to speak, and it's time for her to learn how to master the art of self-regulation.

I'd like to preface my thoughts on this matter by pointing out that illegal, harassing, or hostile behaviors should never be tolerated. Nothing about the modern workplace should cause an employee to feel unsafe, marginalized, unappreciated, disrespected, bullied, manipulated, harassed, gaslighted, or discriminated against for illegal or unfair reasons. This does not necessarily mean that higher authorities should be called to intervene for every instance of discomfort. In fact, part of being a professional is knowing how to advocate for yourself and engage in difficult conversations when they become necessary. But as someone who's suffered mightily over his career at the hands of toxic colleagues and supervisors, I can assure you that self-advocacy and the reporting of egregious behavior should occur whenever they are deemed to be justified. When in doubt, involve persons in your organization, usually HR professionals, who are trained and prepared to give you assistance when you need it or want it – assuming your own supervisor is unable or unwilling to help you. The more emotional you feel about the situation, the more justified you are in seeking assistance.

Thankfully, most of the things that frustrate employees at their places of work are not examples of illegality or gross misconduct. They are frustrations that require diplomacy, patience, and perspective to negotiate. But it's important to understand that all employees in all organizations have frustrations. Those who deal with them successfully are those who've learned to stay focused on their personal and professional goals no matter what happens in their work environments. As much as possible, your sense of progress and professional relevance should be decoupled from and independent of what other people do or say. If you can accomplish this – and I'm not suggesting that it's always easy - it becomes impossible for anyone to deprive you of your sense of well-being, because it remains securely in your own hands.

It also helps to learn how to just ignore something long enough for you to forget about it. Time, as they say, does heal wounds. As scientists, we tend to be very logical creatures and we are easily frustrated by stimuli that don't make sense. And, as a group, we are notoriously introverted, which makes it harder for us to confront people who we believe have wronged us, wronged someone else, or wronged our laboratory.

In my role as a coach, I want to remind you of something I tell my clients often. There are few workplace problems that cannot be solved by a good chat between two or more reasonable people. When things get difficult, be reasonable in your approach to the situation and be willing to sit down and discuss it with whomever else is involved. Often times, that is all it takes to solve even the most vexing problems.

# 5

## Career Doubt

Forensic science is a difficult profession. The fact this book is being written and that you are perhaps referring to it in your attempts to solve a problem are evidence of the challenges inherent to working in this field. Especially when the aforementioned honeymoon period comes to an end, many forensic scientists wonder if they have chosen the right career. Assuming one begins his forensic science career in his early to mid 20s, he may begin to ponder other career options in his late 20s or early 30s while he is still young and possibly without a family to support. The career doubts he experiences may arise from any number of factors or combinations thereof – many of which are discussed on these pages. He may feel burnt out from having worked in the same unit or discipline for several years. He may feel frustrated with case backlogs and high turnaround times that prevent his work from making a difference. He may be struggling on the witness stand and feel unable to get comfortable in his role as an expert witness. Maybe he feels underpaid. Or perhaps he just doesn't like his supervisor or the people with whom he works. He has lots of reasons for not being happy.

If you ever find yourself ruminating about what career you should be in, I'd like you to keep a few things in mind that will help you work through the many conflicting emotions you will feel.

First, ask yourself some probing questions about the life you want to be living, what kind of home you want to have, what kind of car you want to drive, what state or city you want to be in, what people you want to have around you, what kinds of leisure activities you want to enjoy, and where you want your children to grow up, if this applies to you. I bring this up because people have funny ways of blaming their careers or their employers for things that feel incomplete in their *personal* lives. As you consider these life questions, it is equally important that you discuss your thoughts and feelings with people you trust and who know you well. If some of your doubts are unreasonable, they are more likely to be honest with you than you might be with yourself. It is quite possible that you are in the perfect job and in the perfect field but that some mental and emotional work needs to be done on the personal side of life. You've likely been working very hard to establish your professional presence and build your expertise. How much time have you spent taking care of you?

Before you go looking for another job or start house-hunting in another state, ask to speak with someone you trust in a position of higher authority or stature at your laboratory, and don't be scared to do so. Whether they realize it or not, your laboratory's leaders get paid to care how their employees are doing and what things can be done to retain the unique talents and attributes that make you valuable to the team. Do not mention that you are looking for another job or that you are considering resigning. This will be taken as an insult, and justifiably so. Nor should you complain about what's bothering you. Instead, share what it is that you hope to accomplish or what you want. For example, you might say, *I really appreciate the opportunity I have to come to work here every day and be part of this team, but I'm looking for some ways to freshen things up a bit, and I could use some help.*

Whatever you do, avoid putting your employer in the position of trying to compensate for personal challenges or doubts that are outside of its control. It's *your* job to worry about your personal life, so confide in personal friends, confidantes, or family for these kinds of issues. If you are working in Boston and feel a strong pull to move back to your home in Seattle, don't burden your Boston team with professional demands aimed at assuaging your Seattle aspirations. They won't be able to do it and will begin to resent you for putting them in that position. If you feel that your wages are lower than what you deserve, but they are internally equitable when compared to others in your laboratory, that too places you at risk of making demands that cannot reasonably be met.

Below I'd like to present 25 questions that I encourage you to ask yourself for the purpose of assessing whether or not forensic science is still a good career choice for you. Write down your answers and associated thoughts in a notebook so that you can review or modify them later. My goal here is to help you explore your feelings and accelerate your return to a state of mind that is marked by gratitude, joy, and peacefulness.

1. Do I enjoy working in a laboratory?

2. Do I enjoy working in government?

3. Is the field of criminal justice of importance to me?

4. Do I find meaning being closely connected to law enforcement?

5. How much time and energy have I invested so far in the building of my current subject-matter expertise?

6. What people would be very sorry to see me leave my current position, or to leave the profession of forensic science entirely?

7. What people would I miss if I left my current position, or if I left the profession of forensic science entirely?

8. Is courtroom testimony a satisfying experience for me?

9. Although my level of pay may not be exactly where I want it to be, is it reasonable compensation for what I do, how long I've been doing it, the hours I work, the facility in which I work, the location in which I live, the people I get to work with, and the amenities and opportunities to which I have access?

10. Does my job give me an opportunity to learn new things and apply them in the meeting of my professional responsibilities?

11. Does my job afford me the opportunity to have interesting conversations with people I respect?

12. Does my job afford me the opportunity to find creative ways to solve problems?

13. Are there people here at work that I am justified in calling my friends?

14. Do I have the tools to do my job well?

15. Are there people here at work who genuinely care about me?

16. Thinking about the people at work I don't like, do they *really* cause me any damage or serious hardship?

17. Does my work make a difference?

18. Am I professionally relevant?

19. Does my opinion matter here at work?

20. If I stay in my current job or with my current employer, what things can I do in the next 12 months to reignite my enthusiasm?

21. Do I meet new and interesting people on a regular basis?

22. If I was doing the exact same job with the exact same people but in a location more to my liking, how would that make me feel?

23. If I was doing the exact same job in the exact same location but with people I really liked, how would that make me feel?

24. If I was working in a completely different profession but with the exact same people and in the exact same location, how would that make me feel?

25. How much of a loss would it be for me to completely start my career over again?

In those moments when you consider making a major professional change, you have to be clear about what it is you are chasing. If you are not, you will likely find yourself coping with the same feelings of doubt and deprivation that haunted you before. Again, asking yourself some simple questions goes a long way toward creating the clarity you need:

- What is it that I *really* want?

- What is *really* making me feel dissatisfied?

- Who or what is standing in the way of my joy in life?

- Do I *really* deserve something that I am not receiving?

- Could a reasonable person, knowing everything about my life and career, conclude that I have a lot to be thankful for?

- What choices am I making that are causing me to get in my own way?

- What destructive thinking habits are causing me to punish myself with feelings of doubt and displeasure?

If you are surprised by the effort I am making to have you assess the wisdom of changing jobs or careers, there is a good reason for it. The time one spends in the same job, the same organization, or the same occupation carries with it great value, something that should not be thrown away hastily. It tends to be much easier to see the value of making a change than it is to see its risks. Leaving your current position, especially if you change careers entirely, is never something to take lightly, and you should deliberate heavily with people you know and trust. Having doubts is something reasonable people do. Questioning those doubts is something *great* people do.

# 6

## Case Backlogs

When forensic science laboratories lack the resources needed to keep pace with the demand for their services, a situation arises when the number of cases coming into the laboratory becomes larger than the number of cases being completed. As a result, *case backlogs* develop in one or more of the laboratory's work units. As the cases being worked by the scientists become older and older, the interval of time between the original submission of evidence and the final reporting of the testing results becomes longer and longer. This interval is called the *turnaround time*. When turnaround times rise, police officers and prosecutors responsible for investigating and adjudicating these cases must go without forensic results for durations that often exceed their levels of comfort. Judges, too, become angry when forced to delay proceedings because the forensic work has yet to be completed.

Of equal concern to me, however, is the psychological and emotional impact that case backlogs have on scientists. It is nothing short of demoralizing when a forensic scientist feels that her work has less relevance to the criminal justice system. And when turnaround times rise significantly, the results produced by forensic laboratory employees lose some of their relevance.

There are a couple of things to understand about case backlogs in forensic science laboratories that will help you, the forensic scientist, think about them in a healthier way. First, backlogs are not always the result of resource scarcity. In fact, they are often the result of the undisciplined and uninformed submission of evidence by police investigators who don't understand the laboratory's policies or don't know how to discern between high-value evidence and low-value evidence. It is therefore good laboratory practice to administer training programs for police personnel to help them focus on high-value evidence that allows cases to be solved without causing the forensic science laboratory to waste its precious time and resources.

Second, overtime is not always a wise approach to reducing backlogs. As I've discovered over the years, people forced or encouraged to work overtime tend to slow their pace during normal work hours to conserve energy for the working of overtime. As a result, the laboratory loses production capacity over the standard 8-hour period so that scientists can work extra hours or two in the evening. The result too often is a net loss of production. Overtime, of course, is an effective tool for short-term bursts of productivity when it is needed, but it's costly and sometimes ineffective as a long-term solution to excessive demand.

Finally, every forensic laboratory scientist will one day encounter a backlog. It is important to remember that the backlog is not a *scientist* problem, it is a *laboratory* problem. Yes, it is always important for scientists to be consummate professionals and put forth a good day's work for a good day's pay, and there is nothing wrong with working a bit harder and faster to catch up, as long as quality and completeness are not sacrificed. But a forensic laboratory scientist can only do what she can do, and she should not allow herself to feel frustrated or heartbroken because turnaround times are high. The best thing to do is encourage discussion about what is happening and participate in the process of finding the right solutions.

# 7

## Excessive Focus on Productivity

There is absolutely nothing wrong with working hard, in fact I encourage it. Hard work is a sign that a person is committed to what he is doing, which makes him more trustworthy and appreciated. Hard work creates opportunities to contribute, to learn, and to be entrusted with new and greater responsibilities in the future. Hard workers, with few exceptions, are *valued* workers.

There is a point, however, when a forensic laboratory scientist's focus on productivity becomes excessive, inflating his vulnerability to error or nonconformance to laboratory policies or procedures. This desire to be hyper-productive can have a variety of origins, not the least of which is a nagging case backlog. It could also be the desire to work lots of overtime as a way to supplement his income. In other instances, the scientist may feel a strong urge to satisfy the requests of investigators or prosecutors. Indeed, hardworking forensic scientists are a best friend to police and prosecutors seeking to bring fast closure to a criminal investigation or proceeding.

Many forensic science laboratories institute work production quotas or standards against which they judge the productivity of their scientists.

Although some scientists bristle at the thought of this, there is absolutely nothing wrong with it. In fact, these quotas or standards tend to benefit the most hardworking scientists by allowing their productivity to be recognized and celebrated, and by setting a threshold after which they may elect to redirect their energies toward other professional interests such as research, continuing education, or simply getting out into the laboratory to mingle with colleagues. Government agencies have a responsibility to monitor their stewardship of taxpayer resources. Work production standards help to make better sense of how competently human resources are being used in the furtherance of the public interest.

As a human being, your energy and motivation are limited. I'd like to suggest that you create a personal monthly plan that sets specific goals for how productive you would like to be in both your casework and other peripheral activities that are of professional interest to you. Then, make it your routine to plan each and every week before it begins. What subpoenas are awaiting? What appointments are on your calendar? Who do you need to call or connect with? What repeating blocks of time can you commit to casework so that you can get into a rhythm and keep your focus with minimal distraction?

It goes without saying that criminal justice is unpredictable, and it is impossible to know ahead of time exactly what things will drop onto your calendar unexpectedly. Adaptability is a core competency in forensic science so making adjustments on the fly is part and parcel to this line of work. But as you improve your ability to plan, you will begin noticing repeating patterns, certain times during each week or month that seem more conducive to certain kinds of activities. As you recognize these patterns, your ability to plan will improve dramatically.

Your goal should be to maintain a reasonable degree of productivity over the course of each month and year, but without unnecessary stress or hardship, and without any loss of quality or completeness. You can do it through planning, discretion, and professionalism.

# 8

## Excessive Focus on Quality

You will never hear me suggest that there's something wrong with work quality in a forensic science laboratory, that is until we discover a lazy or incompetent forensic scientist using quality as a justification to work at a snail's pace. I can't tell you the number of times I've confronted underperforming scientists who refused to work with deliberate speed or maintain a reasonable level of productivity, citing to me a desire to maximize quality and completeness as their justification. This, of course, insults the contributions of those scientists who know how to balance productivity with quality.

Perhaps it's the administrator in me, but I view quality broadly, meaning that quality work is work performed reliably, promptly, without error, and at a reasonable speed. Quality work in forensic science serves the public interest. Few things irritated me more as a forensic laboratory executive than underperforming scientists who cloaked their laziness within a virtuous insistence on being thorough. Snapping an extra 20 photographs of a gun's serial number is more work but does nothing to add value to the investigation. Rewriting your handwritten notes may improve their legibility but doesn't excuse the lack of legibility when the notes were first recorded.

You may detect that this particular issue causes an emotional response for me, and you would be correct in doing so. The reason I feel so strongly about this is because I've encountered it so often, and because the behavior is so deceptive. The problem is not just about a lack of productivity or laziness. It is also about the distortion of truth one must achieve to incriminate quality as being a natural predator to productivity. In the eyes of those scientists who attempted to deceive me and themselves in this way, I could sense an unmistakable lack of commitment to our many stakeholders across the criminal justice system. And that, perhaps, was the most disturbing thing of all.

Over the last 40 years, we've witnessed an unprecedented prioritization of quality in forensic science, beginning with the very first accreditation of a forensic science laboratory by the Illinois State Police in the early 1980s. As we directed more attention and energy toward the preservation of quality, we also became less responsive to the investigating and prosecuting agencies that depend on our work in the early phases of a criminal case. Over time, however, we learned how to recover our responsiveness while continuing to minimize the possibility for error. We did this by focusing more intently on our professionalism as forensic laboratory scientists and administrators, requiring higher levels of education and thoughtfulness among those we select for work in this field.

Your professionalism as a forensic scientist requires that you be able to strike the right balance between quality and productivity. Your primary responsibility is to do no harm to your customers. Your secondary responsibility is to leverage your laboratory's resources to maximize the value you are able to deliver to them. Without question, quality is very important, but quality also requires that one work with all deliberate speed so that your testing results can be reported promptly and completely to your customers.

# 9

## Change

If you take a moment to reflect on all of the technical and scientific capabilities that both you and your laboratory have *today*, it might occur to you that what we now characterize as normal or routine is the result of decades of change, innovation, and risk-taking on the part of those who came before us. We are all the beneficiaries of change yet, for many of us, we grow chronically comfortable with the way things are now, even growing irritated and obstinate at the prospect of having to suffer the indignity of doing something a bit differently.

I think back to the early years of my career and remember how easy and convenient it was to record our incoming cases and evidence with handwritten logbooks. I remember shooting guns into a wooden box stuffed with cotton to collect bullets for testing. It wasn't that long ago, either! I've only been working in the profession of forensic science for less than 30 years and, in some ways, it is unrecognizable from what it was when I started. As human beings, we are engaged in a constant struggle to make things better. As we make things better, new problems arise that motivate us to make things even better yet. It never ends.

In my coaching practice, I often hear my executive-leadership clients complain about employees who refuse to support change initiatives. These stubborn employees seem to reflexively oppose any attempt by management to keep their teams moving forward. Forward progress, of course, is a key ingredient to maintaining professional relevance, so management can't help but be perplexed. Is it fear? Is it a personal dislike of authority? Once a laboratory decides that a project must be undertaken to modify a method, change a way of doing business, or implement a new technological solution, why would any employee resist that? They are getting paid just the same, right? So, what's the deal?

I've come to realize that people do not resist *change*. They resist *irrelevance*. The moment a decision is made to change the way things are done is the moment the-way-things-are-done becomes irrelevant; and some people take deep offense to this even when they know the decision to change is a reasonable one. Admittedly, leaders don't always do the best job of cultivating buy-in from staff members, especially when they are under pressure to act quickly. But any feelings of irrelevance are swept away once people realize that simply embracing the change and actually putting forth an effort to accelerate it makes everyone remarkably relevant. It is one's tendency to resist change, in fact, that makes her irrelevant. And as the change initiative carries out without her support, its eventual implementation and acceptance erodes her professional confidence because she knows she was on the wrong side of the issue. This leaves her feeling chronically irrelevant, which may only worsen her resistance to change in the future.

Never let it be said that you resist change. It stains your reputation as a professional and erodes confidence in your ability to recognize opportunities for improvement. When the opportunity for change arises, be curious about the possibilities it may have for you and your team. Ask questions and even challenge the wisdom of the change, but never portray yourself as posturing. Remember, if you want to maximize your relevance as a professional and as a member of your team, be an enthusiastic agent for change. It's going to happen anyway.

# 10

## Conflict

A conflict is a meeting of minds that don't agree. For those who avoid conflict, the absence of agreement is rarely a problem. It's the *meeting of the minds* that causes stress. After all, if you didn't have to be in the same room or same organization with your intellectual adversaries, there wouldn't be much conflict. But in a professional setting, you are surrounded by people having their own life experiences, their own world views, and their own ambitions. Conflict, therefore, is inevitable.

Unfortunately, the skills needed to engage effectively in conflict seem to be lacking among professionals in occupations that are intellectually demanding – at least in my experience. Perhaps it's because these kinds of occupations require professionals to spend more time in their own heads, lessening the need to socialize and therefore eroding the socialization skills needed to master the art of negotiation. As forensic scientists, we focus incessantly on *things* and *processes* from the moment our careers begin. In doing so, we sacrifice the opportunity to build strong socialization skills – a sacrifice that professionals in more people-oriented fields don't make. But if you are to succeed in maximizing your professional effectiveness, it's necessary to prioritize social skills as part of your professional growth.

Among those who struggle with social skills or consider themselves to be introverted by nature, interpersonal conflict can be especially unsettling. The experience, if not handled well, can leave one feeling demoralized, exploited, disrespected, or just plain incompetent. The result, of course, is a worsening of his sense of self-confidence and a continued deterioration of his conflict-engagement skills.

I want to let you in on a little secret. Your scientific know-how is a powerful resource to be leveraged in disagreements, debates, arguments, or other forms of conflict. But before I explain this a bit further, I want to make an important distinction. I am not talking here about *clashes*. Clashes are interpersonal confrontations that have no redeeming value, usually fueled by strong feelings of anger or fear. A clash is a venting of emotional pressures without any strategic intent behind it. When it happens, the best approach is to announce your desire to remove yourself from it and politely request that it not happen again.

Conflict, however, has strategic value because it provides an opportunity for opposing ideas and perspectives to be contrasted against each other. Sometimes, but hopefully not often, these conflicts can involve intellectual aggressiveness, raised voices, and the occasional harsh word. But the overall experience of engaging successfully in conflict tends to advance a team and its members, while refining the communication and thinking skills of those involved.

More important is the fact that conflict builds trust. This may seem counterintuitive, but people who are effective at conflict engagement are more likely to be transparent with their intentions and thoughts because they know they are capable of handling any scrutiny or criticism that may arise. They are happy to entertain vigorous discussions about things important to them because they are good at it. As a result, their team members *trust* that what they see is what they actually get. Conversely, people who fear conflict or shy away from it are difficult to trust because they are believed to be hiding something.

So, let's take a moment to explore why you, as a scientist, are well suited to engage in conflict. It all begins with your ability to analyze. In my workshops on professionalism and leadership for forensic science professionals, I've long taught a method for successfully engaging in conflict called the ADAPT method. ADAPT is an acronym that stands for *analyze, describe, agree, partner, thank*. By following this method, you can increase your effectiveness at managing conflict to the point that you might actually look forward to it! Think about that – *looking forward* to conflict! Here's how it works.

**Analyze** – the first step is to be clear about what the conflict actually is. What is the *real* – not perceived – nature of the conflict? Clashes tend to result when two or more people have a substantive disagreement but don't know what it actually is. The just *feel* it. As a result, emotions fill the space that should be occupied by analysis. The more complicated the issues are, the more time this will take, but it is worth the effort. Use your scientific skills to analyze the situation as objectively as possible, relying on the help of others if necessary, to produce an accurate picture in your own mind of what's going on. You're not trying to solve the problem at this point, you're just trying to be real about what it is.

**Describe** – when your analysis is complete, it is important to describe the nature of the conflict with your opposing party. There is no need to fight for superiority in this process. All you are trying to do is articulate the results of your analysis. *This is the nature of the conflict as I see it.* This may take a few iterations as I will explain next, but this description is the gateway into the land of effective conflict engagement.

**Agree** – Effective conflict engagement begins, ironically, with an agreement – an agreement about how the conflict should be described. This in itself may take some effort, even before you attempt to resolve the conflict. Simply agreeing on exactly what the nature of the conflict is leads to effective discussion about how to move forward. DO NOT proceed further until you agree on the description of the conflict or you will likely find yourself in a clash. If this matter is really important to you, then take as much time as necessary to arrive at an agreement on how to accurately describe the conflict.

**Partner** – The partnership phase of the ADAPT method is the beginning of searching for a solution. I've picked my words carefully here. You are *searching* for the solution under the assumption that one exists and simply needs to be found. This mindset demonstrates goodwill and an honest desire to arrive at a mutually beneficial solution. To have a conflict with another person is to have a relationship within him. You can only own 50% of it. This means you have to work together to find the solution – a partnership of sorts, and a very important one at that. Of course, you may not get everything you want, but if you can arrive at a solution with which both of you can live, then you succeeded in finding what once was lost. You may not get everything you want, but you are solving the problem and effectively engaging the conflict.

**Thank** – If you've gotten this far - whether or not you successfully resolved your conflict is not material here - you should express your sincere thanks that your conflict partner was willing to give it a shot. This is a gracious gesture that may set the conditions for a successful negotiation in the future.

Becoming an effective negotiator or engager of conflict is recognizing the opportunity that exists within it – even if the experience is potentially uncomfortable or vulnerable to devolving into a clash. As we've discussed here, conflict is good for teams because it allows competing ideas and perspectives to gain attention, and it builds trust as members of a team regard each other as being open and transparent with their thoughts.

Avoid clashes as much as possible but embrace conflict because it's essential nutrition for a healthy team – and a healthy career.

# 11

## Boredom

For someone looking at the forensic laboratory sciences from the outside, it seems unimaginable that a forensic scientist would ever suffer bouts of boredom in such an interesting profession. It's so exciting, right? Well, not always.

When you do something long enough, it loses its ability to trigger the release and reuptake of chemicals in your brain that attach feelings of joyful wonderment like the new things in your life. Over time, even the most interesting profession can become mundane to its practitioners. It is a phenomenon we experience in most aspects of our lives. Things just get old after a while.

Bouts of boredom are to be expected in any profession, and it would be reckless to make major decisions about your career ambitions simply because of one or two bouts of boredom. Often, boredom is a symptom of other problems in one's personal life, professional life, or both. Among the most common, in my opinion, is laziness.

Laziness? you ask. Yep, that's exactly what I'm saying.

As human beings, we get lazy when it comes to actively creating meaning and joy for ourselves in our work and in our lives. We don't, for example, make an effort to interact with our colleagues as we used to. We stop taking the kind of interest in our areas of expertise that we did in the first few years of our careers. We don't read as much; we don't study as much; we stop being curious about things that happen and things we observe in our work. Said another way, it's not that the bored professional no longer enjoys her work; it's that she stopped making an effort to enjoy it. Sure, when she first began working in forensic science, it was new and exciting. The enjoyment came naturally because it was fresh and stimulating. But over time, her senses became dulled by the routines and repeating patterns of the work. She got lazy, failing to make the effort to self-energize and seek out the enjoyment she now craves.

The great thing about forensic science is that it provides so many options and opportunities for scientists to find joy and meaning in the work if they are willing to make it happen. But I'd like to issue a stern warning here, one that comes from both experience and observation; if you limit your opportunities for professional growth to those experiences for which you expect to receive monetary compensation, then you are doomed to fail in meeting your professional potential. My own career, which has exceeded every expectation I ever could've had, was entirely shaped by the things I did and the efforts I made on my personal time to develop unique areas of expertise and knowledge-niches that allowed me to distinguish myself. I certainly don't expect you to make the kinds of sacrifices that I did, but I do encourage you to love your professional life so much that you are willing to blend it, to a reasonable degree, with the rest of your life. There is no separation of personal life from professional life. It's all life. So, make the most of it and you will likely reap rewards that you never could have expected.

And guess what? You will suddenly find that your life as a forensic science professional isn't so boring after all!

# 12

## Collateral Assignments

A collateral assignment is a responsibility that an employee accepts in an organization, but one that is not reflected in his main job description. In forensic science laboratories, a common collateral assignment given to an employee is the role of health & safety manager. In larger laboratories or laboratory systems, this may be a full-time paid position. In smaller laboratories not having the workforce scale needed to justify such a position, the role of health and safety manager will be executed as a collateral assignment, at least initially. Given enough time in the role, a stipend or other form of compensatory reward may be granted, but it will never amount to a paid position. The role will always be *collateral*.

Accepting a collateral assignment is a generous thing to do. Your laboratory benefits from your willingness to contribute above and beyond what is minimally expected of you. You are essentially doing extra work for no pay, putting yourself in a position to be held accountable for satisfactory performance without any tangible reason for doing so – at least on the surface.

In reality, collateral assignments are the stuff from which great careers are made. And they are highly effective at curing those pesky bouts of boredom we discussed in the previous section. More important, however, collateral assignments are a way that government agencies can reward high performers, much the same way private corporations might issue yearend bonuses. A collateral assignment is a bonus of sorts in that it gives an employee the opportunity to expand the breadth of his expertise, which creates opportunities for greater job satisfaction and the ability to compete more effectively for future promotions.

As you might expect, some employees take a rather cynical view of collateral assignments, regarding them as just another way for laboratory administrators to squeeze more work out of them. If they reluctantly accept an assignment, it's not long before they are demanding monetary compensation. Unfortunately, their obstinance signals a lack of both professional maturity and a genuine commitment to support their teams. This toxic mindset will limit the success they have in the careers.

As the director of both a crime laboratory and state laboratory system, I used collateral assignments to successfully reward high performers and to help them maintain their levels of enthusiasm and engagement. Two employees, in particular, to whom I gave collateral assignments several years ago, far exceeded my expectations and actually made far more of the assignments than even I realized possible. So, it should not be surprising that one is now the director of the same county laboratory, while the other is the director of a large federal forensic science laboratory. Both have enjoyed successful, meaningful careers in forensic science, which could have been predicted by how much they committed to those collateral assignments I gave them earlier in their careers.

The opportunity to take on a collateral assignment is something for which every forensic laboratory scientist should be prepared. It is an opportunity that should not be wasted, and it should be recognized for what it is - a reward for being committed and trustworthy. Take advantage of the platform it gives you to show what you can do.

# 13

## Making a Recommendation

You'll know you've arrived as a professional when your opinion matters enough to be heard or considered as part of a formal recommendation or proposal to your laboratory's administration. You may, for example, recommend updates to your laboratory's evidence submission policies. Or perhaps you might propose an innovative use of federal grant funds. It could also be as simple as requesting the approval for you and two colleagues to attend a professional conference out of state, proposing that, upon your return, you and your colleagues will host a half-day information-sharing session with laboratory staff to explain what was learned and why it matters to your team. Whatever it may be, expressing your wishes or ideas as part of a formal recommendation or proposal is something to celebrate and something to take very seriously. You may not get everything you want, but you can certainly use the moment to earn the respect and confidence of your audience.

As a general rule, if your audience is hearing your idea for the very first time, it is probably too soon to be making any formal recommendations or proposals. It's important to engage in casual conversations about important topics or opportunities before going formal.

You want your recommendation or proposal to be heard, and this requires eliminating any distractions to be caused by the element of surprise. If the issue about which you are seeking some form of administrative approval or action is so important to you, then doesn't it make sense that you would have been talking about it earlier? The answer is yes. Unless there is some time constraint or emergency that falls out of your control, formal recommendations and proposals should not come as a surprise to your audience. This is perhaps one of the biggest mistakes technical and scientific people make when practicing the art of persuasion. They have such confidence in their intellectual capabilities that they think through their ideas in great detail before ever telling anyone about it. When it finally comes time to let the cat out of the bag, their audiences are stunned to learn how long the proposed ideas have been secretly percolating. This erodes confidence in the ideas being expressed and minimizes the likelihood of a deal being struck.

A book that had a tremendous impact on me was recommended by my sister, Katie, who is a very successful sales rep in the medical device industry. I was speaking with her one day about how she goes about convincing prospective clients to buy her products and services. Without hesitation she said "John, you need to read the book *SPIN Selling*; it's considered the Bible on how to be successful in sales." Wanting to improve my own skills in the art of persuasion, I purchased the book, authored by Neil Rackham, and read it cover to cover. As expected, it completely modernized my understanding of how to successfully *sell* my ideas to others. When I began teaching leadership and professionalism workshops for my forensic science clients and students, I made some slight modifications to the SPIN method so that it would better meet their needs. I'd like to share that six-step methodology with you now. Anytime you find yourself with an idea for which you hope to gain the approval of those in positions of authority, this approach will amplify your chances of success.

The Art of Persuasion for High-Stakes Professionals

1. **Chat** – Casual conversation is the way people connect and get to know each other. It's the conduit through which ideas are shared and mutually agreeable solutions to problems are discussed. If there is something you wish to formally recommend or propose, whenever possible, it should first be discussed casually without any business pretenses that might otherwise trigger suspicions. By chatting about things informally, you also afford yourself the valuable opportunity to gauge people's sentiments about issues or details relevant to your ideas.

2. **Inquire** – Whatever you propose is likely going to result in a change to the status quo. If your proposal is accepted, it is likely to affect the same authorities from whom you wish to gain approval. Asking questions of these authorities ahead of time allows you to better assess how you might present your recommendation in a way that assuages their fears and, perhaps, actually creates some benefits for them. This is done, of course, through inquiry – asking questions that allow you to better understand the unique needs, hopes, desires, and fears of your audience. If you are looking to recommend a change to the company that provides carrier gasses for your forensic drug chemistry unit, you might ask your director something like "how much has the price of our helium changed over the last 5 years?"

3. **Pitch** – The pitch is not what you may think. In this step, you are not making your proposal. Instead, you are seeking *approval* to develop a more formal proposal about whatever change or initiative you wish to implement. According to Rackham, the pitch should be no more than 3 minutes, during which you quickly explain the problem you want to solve or opportunity you want to leverage, followed by the potential solution you envision.

Your pitch will conclude by asking for approval to gather some information, conduct a bit of research, then report back to the relevant authority with your findings and your official proposal and recommendation. Be clear about how much time and effort you intend to exhaust, and be sure that this is acceptable to the authority.

4. **Research** – I know what you're thinking - why would I want to conduct research when I already know what I want? Maybe you have already done the research. Maybe the optimal solution is already clear. Well, keep in mind that we are following a process that is designed to give you the best chance of success while earning the trust and confidence of the relevant authority. Also, the purpose of this research is not only to confirm what you wish to recommend or propose, but also the best way to do so. This is all part of doing your due diligence and it is an opportunity that should not be wasted. But before we move to the final steps, I want to extend a word of caution here. Your research should be unbiased and provide a reasonable degree of scrutiny to the validity or justification of what you intend to propose. You are scientist so use your scientific sensibilities to help you through this process. Don't simply gather information to support what you've already decided is best because, if you do, it could damage your credibility and ruin your chances of being trusted in the future.

5. **Report** – In this fifth step, you are going to leverage a rhetorical technique aimed at closing the deal. In this step, you are going to refrain from asking or requesting anything. Instead, you are going to *report* to the relevant authority what your research found and what solution emerged as the best option. By now, your research should have helped you decide how best to report your findings, such as in writing, verbally, graphically, or by some

other combination of means. Now, similar to a news reporter breaking a story, you are going to report your findings and proposed course of action in very clear, objective, and factual terms. Your audience should agree with you that the solution you've identified is indeed the right one and in need of implementation. At this point, just as before, you are not going to *ask* for anything. Instead, you are going to open up the discussion to any questions that your audience may have. But right before you do this, you are going to do one more very important thing.

6. **Encourage** – Your goal is to get to YES. Anything in the minds of your audience that might prevent them from giving you their approval is the result of fear or anxiety of some sort. Because the antidote to fear and anxiety is encouragement, close your presentation by offering words of encouragement, anticipating as best you can what might prevent their buy-in. It might sound something like this: *We made a similar attempt to use this vendor four years ago but with disappointing results. Fortunately, the company made major changes to their quality assurance procedures and have regained their footing as a reputable supplier in the forensic laboratory markets. The chances of this being a successful initiative are very high.*

Your credibility and reputation are on the line when you make a formal recommendation or proposal. Similar to how your credibility would be affected if you made an error in casework, reporting bad information or identifying solutions that wind up not working will damage you. Be methodical in how you assess problems, gather information, and report optimal solutions. The result could very well be the preservation of your good name and your ability to earn the future trust of your authorities.

# 14

## Giving a Speech or Presentation

Like many good things in life, giving a speech or presentation during which you share your expertise and perspectives to an audience is filled with potential risks and rewards. How much you mitigate the risks, and how much you enjoy the rewards, depend largely on two things: preparation and attitude.

In my career I've given hundreds of speeches, keynote addresses, and subject-matter presentations. I've spoken to audiences as large as 1,200 and as small as 4. When you do it as often as I have, you begin to notice patterns that tend to strengthen or weaken your performance as a speaker. My goal here is to simply share with you some of these insights so that you can become a confident, effective speaker as quickly as possible. This is not to suggest that I can address all relevant factors influencing the quality of your public speaking in just a couple of pages, but I can emphasize a few foundational principles that distinguish accomplished speakers from those who lose the respect of their audiences within the first minute of a presentation.

First, suppressing the natural feelings of anxiety that arise during public speaking is key. This is done before your event, not during. More than anything else, anxiety associated with public speaking arises as the result of an entirely flawed mindset about the roles of speakers and audiences. Let me explain what I mean by that.

Weak speakers who suffer debilitating anxiety before and during a speaking engagement inflict this pain on themselves with destructive thinking habits that confuse a peaceful, simple experience for being a turbulent, complicated one. They do so by equating the speaking experience with an act of self-defense, where the speaker regards her audience as being on the attack, launching a barrage of judgements and criticisms toward the speaker with incessant fury. It stands to reason, then, that if the audience is on the attack, the speaker's top priority is self-defense. This drains all the joy and satisfaction from the speaking experience, leaving nothing in its place other than toxic feelings of dread.

Effective speakers avoid this inner turmoil by thinking of themselves as being in partnership with the audience. During a speech or presentation, there is an understood objective shared by everyone in the room: valuable information will be exchanged between the speaker and the audience. The audience, therefore, shares as much responsibility for making the speech or presentation successful as the speaker does. The audience must focus, listen, ignore distractions, and extend to the speaker their thanks and understanding. If they choose not to do this, it is not the speaker's fault. The speaker's job is to craft and deliver a message that is worth the audience's effort.

In my leadership classes, I often tell my students that if the members of an audience are willing to give them the courtesy of their time and attention, then they owe it to their audience to deliver a message that is interesting, relevant, and just entertaining enough to avoid being seen as disrespectful. As a scientist, you may find yourself in the position of giving presentations about highly technical subjects. But this does not mean that your presentations cannot be interesting, engaging, and able to hold your audiences' attention for the duration of the event.

Now, let's turn our attention to preparation. The success of your speech or presentation will depend on how well you prepare yourself. I'm not going to spend much time here on the actual preparation of your content, such as your notes, memorized or scripted comments, and any images you might project onto a screen. Just know that you should practice several times so that your presentation flows as naturally as possible. Also be familiar with the audio/visual equipment you will use, and get to your event location early so that you can confer with event organizers and support staff. Ask if you can visit the room or stage from which you will speak so that you can get a feel of the environment. I still do this after so many years of public speaking. It makes a big difference.

Your preparation must also address your goal of suppressing any anxiety that might weaken your performance. Here is a list of things that can dramatically reduce your body's stress response:

- Avoid sugar or sweets for at least 48 hours prior to your event
- Avoid greasy or other unhealthy foods 48 hour prior to your event
- Avoid alcohol at least 48 hours prior to your event
- Avoid or reduce your caffeine intake on the day of your event
- Just before your event, spend 15-20 minutes or more on deep breathing exercises to activate your parasympathetic nervous system.
- Exercise before your event to dissipate stored energy
- Sit quietly and breathe calmly in the minutes just before your speech or presentation.

And finally, here is the good news about anxiety. Once you begin to speak, the left side of your brain that controls executive functions will kick in, suppressing the right creative side of your brain that likes to imagine all the bad things that are going to happen during your talk. Be bold. To give a speech or presentation means that you've earned it!

# 15

## Feeling Stuck in Your Position

One of the great HR challenges in forensic science is making meaningful career paths available to scientists in laboratories who don't have too many paths available. Especially for the scientist who doesn't feel an urge or desire to promote into a management position – the position of forensic scientist can, at times, create feelings of employment claustrophobia. *Where do I go from here? Am I going to be doing the same work forever?*

Generally speaking, this feeling of being stuck from time to time is normal and not something to panic about. And just because you're feeling stuck doesn't necessarily mean that your laboratory or its administration are doing something wrong. HR professionals have long regarded the 5 to 7 year mark as being the point at which employees begin to feel some emotional fatigue after being in the same position or the same type of position without any significant change. Different employees have different needs with regards to freshening up their career activities. But in my experience as a professional coach, I have found that, indeed, many people would benefit from a job change. They are feeling stagnant and are no longer growing as professionals. They feel an itch to do something different, even if it means sacrificing all that they have built and could continue to build in their current jobs or with their current organizations. There, of course, lies the key to solving this frustrating puzzle. They need to start *building* again.

Let's make something clear. You are *not* stuck. You likely have a good job in what is a very honorable profession. It is doubtful that you are forced to work 60-80 hours a week as do some professionals. Chances are that you are able to make a reasonably good living. Every day you spend in your current job is an opportunity to become better at it, to deepen the relationships you have with the members of your team, and to earn some of the legacy benefits, such as increased personal leave time and internal organizational influence, that come with longevity. There is not a forensic laboratory around every corner, so to leave your place of employment may require you to relocate.

There is nothing I can write here to specifically coach you on your career options because I don't know you personally and I don't know what circumstances you are facing. What I can say with confidence, however, is that if you are feeling bored or stuck in your position, it is possible that you are not making an effort to deepen your professional knowledge and expand your professional impact to the degree you could be. It is possible that you are "floating" and need to get curious again about things and possibilities in your professional sphere of influence. Ask yourself these questions as a way to initiate a conversation with yourself: *What relevant knowledge about my area of expertise or my work is eluding me because I am not making the effort to seek it out? In what professional relationships could I be investing more time and effort? What continuing educational experience might help break me free of this feeling of being stuck? If a promotion is a possibility for me in the future, what can I do now to prepare myself now?*

If you decide, however, that your current position does not and cannot meet your personal and professional needs, then it's time to move on. Use your personal time at home to look for other options.

# 16

## Compensation Frustration

It's nearly impossible to get through a career without encountering moments when you feel that your wages are not where they should be. You feel underpaid, or perhaps you feel others within your organization are *over*paid and, therefore, you feel that the situation is unfair to you. Frustration with your compensation means that you are comparing your compensation with that of others and feeling disenfranchised. It is very possible, of course, that your wages are, in fact, too low. But it's important to understand some basic principles about compensation that may help you evaluate your own wages with more clarity and accuracy.

It is not the ultimate goal of your employer to ensure that your wages are kept at a specific level at a specific time. In the administration of compensation, the goal of every employer is *equity*. There are two kinds of equity: internal and market. *Internal equity* is the state of keeping the wages of employees within an organization fair and reasonable with due consideration to everyone's position, complexity of responsibilities, seniority, qualifications, professional effectiveness, and other factors that are deemed relevant. *Market equity* is the state of keeping an organization's compensation competitive within a particular job market, so the organization is able to retain its talent and attract qualified candidates to vacant positions that have been publicly posted. It is absolutely impossible for your employer to keep everyone's wages 100% equitable 100% of the time, and it will make you look foolish and immature if you vocalize any expectation that it does so. Although very subjective, it is my opinion that a forensic scientist's wages should be made as equitable as possible every 3 years. As a forensic scientist, this means you may have to be patient from time to time. As long as your wages are reasonable considering all relevant factors, then you might be well-advised to either wait it out for a while or politely and professionally express your desire, at some point in the near future, to have your wages reviewed for internal and market equity.

To the extent that you wish to initiate a conversation with your employer about your current level of compensation, there are some other details you should keep in mind. Your employer is not actually concerned with *your* wages alone. In return for your professional contributions, your employer pays you what are called *total rewards*, which is the combined value of your wages, benefits, terms of employment, and conditions of employment. This value is usually much higher and more difficult to calculate than what employees realize. For example, the value of working in a brand new, state-of-the-art forensic science laboratory is much higher than working in an old, outdated facility that was originally built as a public library in 1962, but was later converted into a forensic science laboratory in 1975. This value or lack thereof factors into the total rewards equation and is part of an overall plan that must be funded and administered by your agency. Of course, the value of some benefits depends on where you are in your career. As a young forensic scientist, there is great value in working in a laboratory that has a high case volume because it allows you to develop your forensic casework expertise much faster. To an older scientist, the opportunity to do some research, provide training, or hold offices in relevant professional organizations may be more valuable. Monetary benefits such as high-quality health insurance, personal leave time, and the availability of tuition reimbursement are critical as well.

As discussed earlier in this book, among the most valuable nonmonetary benefits that an employer can provide is the opportunity for employees to learn and grow as professionals. The funds that your laboratory spends on your continuing education, professional training, and professional networking must be factored into your calculations. So too must the work environment and organizational culture in which you work. As you can see, not all of the value you derive from your job is monetary, and you must give serious consideration to nonmonetary factors if you ever want to have an intelligent conversation about compensation with your supervisor, HR staff, director, or your other laboratory administrators.

Okay, so I'd like to take a moment now to express a thought that you may recognize as being a repeating theme throughout this book – that your view of your professional circumstances is heavily biased by things going on in your *personal* life. Generally speaking, HR research has shown over and over again that employees don't leave their jobs or grow discontent simply because of compensation. In fact, employees have a remarkable capacity for demonstrating patience and understanding when it comes to their pay. But, as we've discussed in previous sections, boredom and feelings of being stuck in one's position can do damage to how an employee feels about his job, including his compensation – even if that compensation is equitable.

Finally, among the top reasons that employees become disenchanted with their jobs, including their compensation, is poor leadership or supervision. As I shared with you in the introduction of this book, I endured the personal and professional effects of significant leadership dysfunction in my career and even changed jobs and relocated my family because of it. When management practices, either individually or culturally, become dysfunctional enough, there is not enough money in the world to make you feel better. As a result, you will experience chronic frustration with your pay. In the next section, I will give you some things to think about when it comes to working with your direct supervisor or managers.

In the meantime, whether you are frustrated with your current levels of compensation or not, it is incumbent upon you as a professional to be and remain aware of the total rewards that you enjoy as the result of being employed in your current position and within your current organization. I will go so far as to argue that if you feel bored or stuck in your current job, as we've discussed previously, it is possible that you are failing to appreciate or account for all the monetary and nonmonetary benefits that your job brings you. In the absence of this gratitude, you will tend to slouch emotionally, looking in the wrong places for the satisfaction you are seeking. Job satisfaction is not something that your employer can give you. It is something you must create for yourself by making the necessary effort.

But if compensation is truly at issue, then there are conversations to be had and you must prepare for these conversations with your employer by first having a conversation with yourself about what is actually missing. Is it *really* about compensation? Is there something else going on that is affecting how you feel about your pay?

As your coach, I'd like to have you spend a full week doing a simple self-reflection exercise. For two days, let's say Monday and Tuesday, I'd like you to write out all of the things that you like about your job and the value you derive from it. During those two days, take a few moments here and there to record things you appreciate or find valuable. I'm asking you to do this over two days because it is impossible to do it in one sitting. Things will pop into your consciousness during those two days that you will want to capture. Take a day off, then take another two days to write out what you don't like about your job or what you feel is draining value away from you or your career potential. When you have your lists completed, sit down and review them. Some people like to create their own scoring system to help them gauge the weight or significance of each item. Do whatever works for you; just make sure you are building your awareness of what's really going on.

# 17

## Being a Partner to Management

Unless you work as a private consultant or in a similar capacity, you likely have a direct supervisory authority, or supervisor, to whom you report. Above your supervisor in the chain of command is a network of other supervisory authorities with increasing levels of responsibility, including a single authority who serves in a top executive role. This network of decision-makers is responsible for you and everything you do, so their opinion of you matters. What also matters is the effort you put forth to keep those opinions of you as high as possible, and to do so responsibly, ethically, and legally. Your direct supervisor, in particular, represents your employer in the business she conducts with you. And she represents you (at least she should) in the business she conducts with your employer.

Among the worst things that can happen in this kind of employee-employer relationship is for the employee to think of himself as the child and for the supervisor to think of herself as the parent. When this happens, the quality of the relationship becomes compromised as communication and collaboration weaken.

So, what should the employee-employer relationship look like? What should it feel like? Well, to be candid, it should be and feel like a *partnership*, as if the employee and his supervisor are co-owners of the organization and are equally responsible for its success. Mutual support, communication, the sharing of ideas and information, and mutual encouragement should the norm. These, unfortunately, don't happen in child/parent-like workplace relationships because the employee is excessively focused on subordinating himself to the supervisor and the supervisor is focused on maintaining dominance.

In making mention of partnerships as a healthy priority in the relationships between supervisors and their employees, I recognize and respect the elevated *decision-making* responsibilities that supervisors have. I also recognize and respect the responsibility employees have to honor and support the decisions of their supervisors, once they are made. But it's the intervals of time between the decisions where the partnership must flourish. It is between the decisions that communication takes place and mutual respect are reinforced. Supervisors, after all, don't spend that much time making critical decisions that require them to exercise dominance over subordinate employees.

As a professional forensic scientist, you should look for legitimate opportunities to be supportive and understanding of your supervisor. Think of yourself as an equal, but with respect for the responsibilities that your supervisor has. Do what you can to make your supervisor's job easier and steer clear of behaviors and performance problems that distract your supervisor from directing her energy toward the strategic objectives of your laboratory or laboratory system. Your supervisor should be genuinely glad that you are part of the staff, and it is your responsibility to give her legitimate reasons to feel that way. Even if you don't like your supervisor very much or find that you have conflicting opinions, you can still find ways of contributing to your relationship with her – as a trusted partner.

# 18

## Supporting your Parent Agency

Although most forensic science laboratories in the United States fall under the executive control and responsibility of a law enforcement agency, even these arrangements can have different forms and structures. In Pennsylvania and Michigan, for example, the state forensic science laboratories fall under their respective departments of state police. In Utah, the state crime laboratory director reports to a department of public safety. In Palm Beach County, Florida, the crime laboratory is operated by the sheriff.

Some publicly funded forensic science laboratories, however, do not fall within police agencies at all. This includes the laboratories of the commonwealth of Virginia, the city of Houston, Texas, and Washington, D.C. Regardless of how your organization is structured and funded, you likely have a parent agency through which your laboratory's funding and executive decision-making flow. It is also likely that the executive leaders of your parent agency have never worked in forensic science and know very little about the profession. This, at times, can cause friction and frustration.

No, your parent agency may not know much about forensic science, but it's nonetheless a legitimate organization with legitimate priorities and a legitimate mission. As a forensic science professional, it is your job and the job of everyone working in your laboratory to make sure that you remain committed to the priorities and mission of your parent agency. That the leaders of your parent agency may not always seem to understand or even support your forensic science operations is not a justification to disengage.

As scientists, we tend to think highly of the work we do and the intellectual brainpower we have to do it, which causes us to think highly of ourselves and our opinions. Few things will cause your laboratory to lose the respect and support of your parent-agency leaders more than behaving with righteous indignation, as if you are entitled to something. I've seen this mistake made on too many occasions with significant long-term damage done. Just as I've encouraged you to be a partner to your direct supervisor, I also encourage your laboratory to position itself as a valuable and supportive partner to the leaders of your parent agency. It is often the only way you can ensure the maximum degree of support and funding you need to do your work the way it needs to be done.

Your laboratory director is ultimately the person responsible for negotiating the many issues that arise between your laboratory and its parent agency. Support him as much as possible and avoid the temptation to make judgements about how he does it. You are not privy to all of the relevant dynamics that influence the nature of this relationship. My guess is that, whatever your own thoughts and opinions are, your director is doing the best he can. As a former laboratory director and system director, I can attest to the complexity of the challenges, opportunities, disagreements, and expectations that influence a forensic laboratory's relationship with its parent agency. I also know what it feels like when laboratory staff adopt strong opinions about things about which they know very little. Be calm and reasoned in your thinking about your parent agency and be supportive of its leaders and its overarching mission. Trust me, it's good for your career.

# 19

## Civilian Discrimination

Civilian employees are those who have no official constitutional authority legally granted to them through established public institutions. As part of their jobs, civilians do not carry guns and do not wear badges. Civilians do not hold military ranks such as sergeant or lieutenant as police officers do, and they have no powers of arrest, prosecution, or judicial rule. Civilians are often employed by constitutionally recognized agencies and may be permitted to act on their behalf, but civilians have no inherent constitutional power of their own.

It is an unfortunate and sometimes shameful reality in many – but not all, of course - police organizations that civilian employees are treated like second-class citizens. The relationships among sworn officers in today's police culture are very fraternal and self-protective. And, although civilian employees make up approximately 30% of all employees in police agencies in the United States, according to FBI statistics, civilians are not members of police officer unions and are not considered part of the "family."

In my popular 3-day workshop titled *Administration and Leadership Academy for Law Enforcement Civilians*, I teach my students how to function effectively in police culture. I encourage civilians, including you if the title applies, to be mindful of and confident in the knowledge, skills, and abilities they have to do their jobs well. For you the forensic scientist, the education, training, and experience that allow you to do the complex and intricate work for which you are responsible is something to be respected. Being discriminated against because you are *only a civilian* is something you may encounter in your career.

When this happens, you must remind yourself of the value you deliver to your employer and to our society. You are important and you deserve to be treated as such. I recommend that you not initiate clashes with police officers as it will do you no good, especially if they are part of your chain of command. I do, however, recommend that you stand tall, be confident, and act like you are deserving of respect. Police officers, interestingly, are keen observers and readers of people. If they detect that you lack confidence, they will be less likely to have confidence in you. If they sense you are questioning yourself and your abilities, so will they.

Most police officers are very kind and reasonable and they appreciate the role civilian employees play in our criminal justice system. Others, however, can be remarkably hostile and discourteous towards civilians. If you experience this for yourself, be professional and resolute in your verbal and physical communication. Your job is to carry out your responsibilities, not to correct the behaviors of other professionals who are not under your control.

Being discriminated against because you are a civilian can be very frustrating and hurtful. Overcome it by continuing to develop yourself and your professional skills. One thing that is rarely discriminated against is competence.

# 20

## Workplace Injury

Working as a forensic firearms examiner, as I did for many years, comes with its own risks. I recall the day I sprayed oil into the ejection port of a rusty pistol only to have the oil and bits of rust spray back directly into both of my eyes. Our laboratory's health and safety manager was close by and helped me to the eyewash where I rinsed out my eyes for several minutes. She then documented the incident and filed a report with our office. I was, of course, embarrassed beyond words. Oh, yes, I was also the laboratory director.

Workplace injuries happen and one will likely happen to you at some point in your career. Most, thankfully, are minor and only require first aid to treat. From time to time, more serious incidents happen in forensic science laboratories resulting in injury requiring medical treatment such as chemical spills or splashes, bad cuts, pokes with needles or syringes, trips and falls, and so forth. Among the worst, of course, is the unintentional discharge of a firearm resulting in a gunshot wound. Although this is very rare, it has happened in forensic science laboratories before, and it will likely happen again.

The reporting of workplace injuries and the compiling of statistics on such injuries is an important priority in the United States. The Occupational Safety and Health Administration (OSHA), as well as the National Institute for Occupational Safety and Health (NIOSH) take very seriously the duty of employers and employees to report injuries when they occur. You and your laboratory share this responsibility.

The more difficult question that frequently arises is, *Do I have to report very minor injuries such as small scrapes or cuts that require very little treatment, if any? What about a paper cut?*

Here's what you need to know. You will never hear any responsible or legitimate legal or safety professional tell you that there are certain injuries that you shouldn't report. Promptly reporting ANY injury (report all injuries as soon after occurrence as possible) ensures that you can receive medical treatment and benefits from your employer should the injury cause you to lose work and pay. If you believe that you suffered a workplace injury, then report it. Even a small cut can become the transmission point for a pathogen, and you may not know that you've been infected until later on.

Be extra cautious about injuries caused while you are in contact with the forensic evidence you are testing. Firearm & toolmark examiners, trace evidence examiners, and latent print examiners are at an elevated risk for evidence-related injuries because they work directly with so many different kinds of evidence that come into the laboratory, none of which is disinfected prior to submission. Forensic biologists who work with body fluids are also exposed to risk in the form of bloodborne pathogens.

Consider this your rule – if you suffer a workplace injury of any kind, treat it appropriately, make yourself and your coworkers safe, then report it as quickly as possible to your health and safety manager or other authority responsible for documenting workplace injuries.

# PART 2

Professionalism and Integrity

# 21

## Accreditation Assessments

The accreditation progress is rigorous and challenging for forensic science laboratories and their employees – at least it *should* be. In the early years of forensic laboratory accreditation, onsite inspections, as they were called, took place every five years. Between those inspections the laboratory and its staff went about their business until the time came for the next inspection. The infrequency of the inspections made each one feel like a very big deal. Like planning for a wedding, laboratory administrators and scientists would prepare feverishly to make sure everything was in order, hoping to get through the inspection without any findings. This is not to suggest that between inspections laboratories were doing poor or nonconforming work, but rather to emphasize that accreditation felt like a test you had to pass every five years – something that came and went like a tropical storm.

With the introduction of ISO standards to the accreditation framework, laboratory assessments, as they are now called, occur every four years at a minimum, with periodic surveillance monitoring that takes place on a prescribed schedule. More than ever before, forensic laboratory accreditation is a *way of life*. And as forensic science laboratories have gotten better and better at understanding the requirements and demonstrating conformance to them, the experience of being assessed by a team of strangers is not as shocking as it used to be.

Being prepared for each and every accreditation assessment requires that forensic scientists:
- understand accreditation
- know the requirements
- conform to the requirements
- have the right attitude

Having the right attitude about accreditation is key. It means that you recognize that accreditation is not a discomfort that is *inflicted* upon you and your laboratory against your will. Accreditation is not oppressive. Instead, accreditation gives forensic science laboratories an opportunity to demonstrate that they conform to industry standards designed to minimize the likelihood of error and maximize the likelihood of accuracy. On the other hand, accreditation is not a prestigious award that justifies boasting or ceremonial grandstanding. Being accredited means that your laboratory meets *minimum* standards. As an executive coach, it's my hope that you and your laboratory strive for something more than what is *minimally* required.

Finally, it's important to recognize that innovation and bold leadership have the effect of creating change. Change is good because it represents progress, assuming it is reasonably thoughtful. The more your laboratory changes between accreditation assessments the more likely it is that it's inadvertently slipped out of conformance in some areas. Therein lies the true beauty of accreditation, in my opinion. It provides cover to laboratory administrators and employees who are creative, assertive, and enjoy experimentation. It's just another reason to be thankful for accreditation, not resentful or afraid of it.

# 22

## Attendance at Professional Conferences

Careers in forensic science have been made and destroyed at annual professional conferences. These important events afford us the opportunity to interact with our peers, establish and maintain our network, and continue the building of our subject-matter expertise through learning and discussion. In forensic science, professional conferences are a lifeline that keep our scientific and administrative practices in a continuous state of improvement and evolution.

But here is the problem. Too many forensic science professionals view these events as an escape – a place to get away and unwind. They treat annual professional conferences like a vacation, an opportunity to get out of the laboratory for a while and be with colleagues and friends. And guess what? I felt the same way and still do! But I also understood and understand that my reputation and professional stature depend on how I behave at these events and how I leverage the opportunity to create value for myself and my employer. Professional conferences are a strategic opportunity, not a personal retreat.

Sadly, some young professionals don't handle freedom well. Some older ones don't either, now that I think about it. Especially if they are vulnerable to compulsive behaviors inflamed by alcohol and/or sexual arousal, a professional conference can be the place where professional suicide is committed, where marriages end, and where deep personal embarrassment is suffered. Free of the protective constraints that work and home life naturally provide to so many of us, spending a week on the road with a large group of peers, who also work under the pressures that are inherent to forensic science, creates temptations that the weakest among us may not be able to resist. Even worse, the weakest among us seem to always find each other, which is when trouble *really* begins.

There is absolutely nothing wrong with enjoying yourself at professional conferences. You *should* have fun, and you should enjoy the opportunity they give you to grow as a person and as a professional. Some of my dearest friends, to this day, I met at professional conferences and I rely on them regularly for their advice, perspective, and support. But there are two things I ask you to keep in mind whenever you attend a professional conference. First, it is your responsibility to make the conference professionally valuable to you and your laboratory. Attending a conference is not a benefit; it is a strategic investment that your laboratory makes with the expectation of producing a return on that investment. Pay attention, listen carefully, absorb knowledge, and then bring that knowledge back to your laboratory so that your laboratory can improve, even if just a little bit. Second, keep yourself under control. Have fun, enjoy your peers, but NEVER allow yourself to be seen as succumbing to compulsions. If you fail, you will be astonished at how quickly word will travel through your organization about your behavior and your apparent lack of personal integrity. It will damage your ability to be taken seriously and may erode opportunities you have to assume leadership positions within your organization later on down the road.

A professional conference can be an amazing, rewarding experience for any professional. But it can also be a venue for personal and professional destruction. Don't let that happen to you!

# 23

## Disagreeing with the Conclusion of a Peer

Expert opinions carry no significant weight until they are officially reported to a client. In the forensic science laboratory, the results or conclusions of forensic scientists are officially finalized in a testing report that is issued to the submitting agency or customer. During the analysis and/or prior to the official reporting, however, scientists may seek out each other's input or assistance when the circumstances surrounding the testing of evidence are complicated or confusing. *Hey, can you take a look at this and tell me what you think?* is not an uncommon question in a forensic science laboratory. In fact, I encourage this kind of collaboration because it facilitates conversation and learning.

Sometimes, though, a secondary scientist is required to review the work of a primary scientist in a case. This may be for the purpose of conducting a quality-assurance audit of a case record, known as a *technical review,* or to reexamine one or more items of evidence for the purpose of giving a second opinion, which is known as a *verification* and is also part of the quality-assurance requirements of many laboratories. Although not especially common, situations might arise when the opinion of the secondary or reviewing scientist is not in agreement with the original or primary scientist. In this instance, we have a disagreement between the two scientists.

To be clear, there is nothing wrong with a disagreement like this coming to fruition as long as one or both of the scientists' egos are not so fragile as to be incapable of discussing the matter with professionalism and tactfulness. It may come to pass that after further review one of the scientists comes to realize that he is wrong and, in fact, agrees with his colleague. This takes personal strength to say the least. In other instances, the two scientists may never agree, requiring that the more conservative of the two opinions – the one that is less likely to cause an innocent person to be erroneously convicted – or no opinion at all be reported. "Inconclusive" is a perfectly legitimate result if it is warranted.

Whatever the situation may be, it is vital that both scientists be professional, collaborative, and diplomatic in discussing the matter with each other. Laboratory policies and procedures should be followed carefully. But if egos get in the way and there is any potential for an interpersonal clash to erupt, a laboratory supervisor and/or the laboratory's quality manager should be consulted.

As a forensic scientist, if you ever find yourself in this uncomfortable position, be calm, courteous, and professional. You do not want your working relationship with your colleague to be damaged over it. At the same time, your top priority as a forensic scientist is to ensure that no undue harm is done to the evidence, to the case, or to any of its parties. It is when serious disagreements arise that we get the chance to see just how professional we are. Don't rush anything and don't bully or manipulate your colleague or the situation. Work your way through it carefully, making sure you keep the conversation going until a mutually agreeable and responsible solution is found. Please refer to the ADAPT method in chapter 10.

# 24

## Disagreeing with the Conclusion of a Supervisor

Several years ago, I found myself in what can only be described as one of the most threatening and unsettling situations I've ever experienced. My supervisor, having about 20 more years of experience than me, was unable to identify a questioned toolmark as being made by a suspect tool that was submitted to our unit as part of a routine proficiency test. When both he and my coworker both finally gave up their efforts, it was my turn to work the test. Within about an hour I was able to identify the suspect tool as having made the questioned toolmark. When I sheepishly announced that I had "made the ID," both my supervisor and coworker took turns at the microscope to see it for themselves. "Well I'll be damned," my supervisor chirped before strolling into his office. He hardly spoke a word to me over the course of the next week, and it was the beginning of a deteriorating and sometimes abusive relationship.

I am fundamentally opposed to subordinate employees reviewing the work of their direct supervisors for official quality-assurance purposes. In my view, it is an exercise that is fraught with risk. It takes a remarkably strong and secure individual to take issue with the work of a direct supervisor, especially one prone to being personally offended by it. Trust me, I have done it and it was excruciating. The quality management system of a forensic science laboratory should not depend on superhuman strength to ensure the execution of a reliable review of work, but that is exactly what may be needed if an inexperienced employee finds herself having to potentially point out the mistake of a superior.

At the same time, I have empathy for smaller laboratories that do not have the staffing to comply with my wishes on this matter. It may be that the employee and her supervisor are the only two scientists in the laboratory having the requisite training and expertise. If this is the case for you, and you are the employee doing the review of your supervisor's work, all I can do is encourage you to be strong and resolute in your solemn responsibility of subjecting the work to a complete review or reanalysis as prescribed by your laboratory's quality-management policies and procedures. If you believe that your supervisor made a mistake and that bringing the mistake to his attention is risky, be diplomatic and understanding in how you address the issue. In fact, *you* may be the one who is wrong. Whatever you do, don't summarily judge your supervisor's work as being inaccurate. Simply let him know that you might have found a problem with the case (not a problem with his work) and want to chat about it. Once you get his attention, you can proceed from there. At any time, if you feel that you are being bullied or that your interest in engaging on the issue is being taken personally, stop the discussion and decide on next steps. You may need to involve someone who can mediate or referee the dispute. Again, your primary responsibility is to ensure that no harm comes to the case or its parties and that laboratory policies and procedures are followed.

# 25

## Being Tempted to Lie or Cheat

I know, this section doesn't apply to you, right? You would never lie or cheat – no way! Well, would it surprise you if I, the author of this book and two others, admitted that I would, in fact, lie or cheat? I've testified in over 130 criminal trials – some were death penalty cases. How does it make you feel to hear me reveal such an incriminating admission?

Let's cut to the chase. Both of us would lie or cheat if the circumstances were right. All of us have a circumstantial threshold at which we would do something regretful. And, as I teach in my workshops on professional ethics and integrity, one can only maximize his ethical centeredness if he is willing to acknowledge, accept, and admit that he will certainly lie or cheat if circumstances arise where the desire to engage in misconduct overpowers the desire to do what's right. Sure, he might be a very strong, responsible, and moral fellow who would only lie or cheat under a set of circumstances that are highly unlikely to ever occur. But what if they *do* occur? And what if they arise so slowly that he doesn't even notice it's happening? The answer is, he *will* lie and cheat, then he *will* be shocked when he realizes he did.

Obviously, we're talking about lying and cheating in a professional context where the consequences of the misconduct are potentially severe. This topic is near and dear to my heart because I experienced heartbreak when a routine audit revealed that a respected colleague of mine was stealing money from our laboratory's evidence vault. He was arrested and prosecuted. I never could have seen it coming in a million years. And I am sure that *he* never could have seen it coming in a million years either. But with five children, a troubled marriage, and financial problems that apparently set in, he got to a point where it became a good idea to steal money that didn't belong to him, and to abuse his official capacity as our office's evidence custodian to do it. If I could go back in time and ask him if he would ever do something like that, I am sure his answer would be *HELL NO! ARE YOU CRAZY?!?!?*

As a forensic scientist, you are exposed to temptations. It could be as simple as cutting a few corners during a forensic analysis so that you can get home in time for your son's Friday night football game. It could also be as significant as giving false testimony in court because the defense attorney's challenge to your qualifications seems to be gaining strength. It's silly for me to sit here and implore you to never lie or cheat in your capacity as a forensic scientist, because I know what you'd think. *Of course I would never do such a thing; why would he even say something like that?* Instead, it is better and more constructive for me to encourage you to be very aware of the circumstances that exist in your personal and professional life. Do what you can to avoid ever wanting something so bad that you would do something unethical or criminal to get it. And, if you feel a sinister temptation grabbing a hold of your heart and mind, remove yourself immediately from the situation and seek the support of someone you trust.

If you can't remove yourself from the situation, remind yourself that your reputation, your livelihood, and your freedom are more important than what this one moment of weakness could ever give you.

# 26

## Confronting Misconduct in the Laboratory

Let me be clear about something for a moment. I don't believe you will engage in gross or criminal misconduct in your career. The fact that you are even reading this book suggests that you care about your career and want to be successful in everything you do. You've come a long way and you don't want to tear down what you've built up through your hard work and smart choices. Plus, the chances that circumstances will arise such that you would be sufficiently tempted are very unlikely. But, as I explained earlier, I encourage you to recognize that you are not immune from temptation. It's just a healthier way to think about the subject of ethics and morality.

More likely, perhaps, is the possibility that you might one day catch somebody else doing something unethical, immoral, or in violation of your laboratory's policies and procedures. What do you do then? Confront the wrongdoer? Report her to the laboratory administration? Do nothing at all? Do you even know what options are available to you?

Witnessing unethical or immoral behavior in the workplace puts the observer in a very difficult position, especially if the wrongdoer is in a position of authority. It won't surprise you to hear me say that what you do depends on the situation, but I can share with you some basic principles and considerations that will help you if you find yourself in this most difficult of predicaments.

Generally speaking, if you are smart enough to know that an unethical or immoral act has been committed in your presence, then you are smart enough to judge whether or not the misbehavior was dealt with appropriately. Therefore, it is not always good enough to report a wrongdoer to a higher authority in your workplace. The law doesn't care about your respect of workplace ranks or titles. What the law cares about is preventing harm to others. As a witness, you now have high authority of a special sort. Bestowed upon you is the solemn obligation of making sure that the behavior and similar behaviors won't likely happen again, and that reasonable efforts are made to ensure harmed parties are made whole. You may have an ethical obligation to seek assurances that reasonable actions were taken in response to the misconduct. If nothing is done or the matter is swept under the proverbial rug, future misconduct could potentially be blamed on you.

At the low-end of the misconduct scale, I've always felt that wrongdoers should be confronted immediately and reported to a supervisor. In more serious situations, immediate confrontations may provide an opportunity to destroy incriminating evidence, as was the case in a very serious situation I dealt with several years ago. Thankfully, with the prevalence of mobile phones, it is easy to take pictures that can be used to confirm or dismiss that misconduct took place.

At a minimum, think of witnessing misconduct as being a kind of injury. Just as you would report an injury, report any suspicious behavior or outright misconduct. If you don't like how the matter is being handled, take it to the next level of authority, doing so until you feel you've met your own ethical and moral obligations. Under no circumstance should serious misconduct ever be allowed to stand.

# 27

## Harassment by Review

Among the more childish behaviors I've ever witnessed in the forensic science laboratory is the use of quality-assurance reviews to harass or intimidate other employees. Reviewers have the authority to kick-back or delay the release of a testing report when it is determined that there is even a minor error or something otherwise wrong with the analysis documentation or draft report. This compels the original scientist to address the issue, make the necessary corrections (if any), then reissue a draft report for yet another review. It's better to get it right the first time.

Unfortunately, the power granted to a reviewer can be easily abused. In the worst instances, the release of a report might be delayed for reasons that have little or no significance or legitimacy. In one instance that I recall, a DNA testing report was delayed during review because the reviewer didn't like the way a sentence was structured. When the original scientist came to me to complain, I looked at the report and saw that the sentence in question was perfectly acceptable. This led me to suspect that the reviewer was intentionally seeking to inconvenience the original scientist.

Several years ago, one forensic scientist for whom I was hired to provide professional coaching told me of a declining culture in her laboratory. When I asked her to give me an example, she explained a troubling situation in which two scientists were literally feuding with each other by nit-picking each other's work and kicking it back for revision with alarming frequency. The supervisor of the unit was so busy that the misbehavior went unnoticed for quite some time.

Of course, there are two sides to this dispute on which you can potentially find yourself. If you are the reviewer, I urge you to never abuse the review process. It weakens the culture of your laboratory by gaming your quality management system. Any behavior that makes a mockery of quality management will have very serious long-term effects. Only kick back work if there is a glaring problem, error, or oversight that indicates a mistake was made, or that a misspelling or serious word usage problem appears in the report. As always, comply with your laboratory's policies and procedures, but don't deprive your laboratory's customers of their opportunity to receive prompt service.

On the other hand, if you are the original scientist and your work is being kicked back for reasons that seem capricious or arbitrary, do not respond emotionally. Be very calm and business-like as you politely approach your reviewers to challenge their judgement. If you disagree with a decision to kick back work and you have a solid basis upon which to stand, then make this very clear. You may ask something like, *Is it necessary for our customer's receipt of this report to be delayed because of your review in this case?* If the behavior continues, there will need to be a lengthy discussion with your supervisor and other staff members about the possibility that your review processes are being abused. Keep in mind, however, that some scientists are hopeless perfectionists and can't help themselves, meaning that their reviews are not acts of malice but are instead acts of compulsion. A good conversation and possibly a few updates to your quality review procedures might be all that is needed to fix this problem for good.

# 28

## Making an Error

We aren't supposed to make errors in forensic science. It's culturally and professionally reviled, tantamount to a mortal sin. I'm not talking about spelling errors in reports or the occasional mistake that causes no real harm other than some lost time. I'm talking about coming to a scientific conclusion that turns out to be wrong, or failing to conduct your analysis in compliance with laboratory procedures - something that embarrasses you in front of your coworkers and potentially damages the confidence your laboratory has in your abilities.

Obviously, there are degrees of error. Some are very minor, and some are catastrophic. Some occur in the laboratory, while some occur on the witness stand while answering difficult questions. An entire book can be written about how to handle the most serious errors. What's important to note, however, is that the practice of forensic science and the application of its many quality assurance measures makes serious errors impressively unlikely. When they do happen, it is more likely than not that the offending scientist is competent but was rushing or was simply careless.

Making a serious error can feel like the earth stopped spinning. Of course, you didn't mean to do it – it just happened – at least that's how it feels. The worst thing you can do – and I mean the WORST thing you can do – is be defiant or self-righteous in your response. As a laboratory administrator, I always felt like I could stomach an unintentional error on the part of one of my scientists; and I saw it as a learning moment for the scientist and a teaching moment for the supervisor. What I could not stomach was behavior that suggested a lack of remorse or embarrassment. Remorse and embarrassment are emotions that competent scientists will feel upon realizing they made a mistake. Defiance and self-righteousness are displays of grandstanding that signal a lack of professional seriousness and a disregard for how the error effects other people in the laboratory.

If, one day, you learn that you made an error. These are the kinds of things you should say and questions you should ask:

- *I feel horrible, I can't believe this happened.*

- *I understand that we need to figure out why this happened; I'd like to help if I may.*

- *Is there anything I can do to help rectify the problem?*

- *I don't want anything like this to ever happen again. Please know that I am completely open to remedial training or coaching.*

- *Correcting this problem is important to me.*

Of course, if you know why the error happened, you would be wise to communicate it as soon as possible. At the same time, be mindful of the possibility that some other factor or person was involved in some capacity. Either way, the goal of the laboratory is not to punish you. Instead, the goals are to prevent the error from happening again and repair any damage that may have been caused. Just because you made the error does not mean that you cannot be part of the solution. If there was ever a time to be collaborative, this is it.

# 29

## Loss of Self Confidence

Confidence is the blissful feeling of buoyancy you feel when you know what you're doing and you feel like you have control over what's going on in your life – both personally and professionally. Confidence is gained through experience, learning, experimenting, and succeeding. When you have it, you feel good and strong. When you don't, you feel weak and exposed.

Confidence ebbs and flows over the course of our lives. We may find that we have it for long periods of time, and then we seem to lose it. As life marches on, circumstances change, and so do aspects of our lives. You may be completely confident in your current job, for example, but if you get promoted to a managerial position, you may find that your confidence drops substantially. Changing employers or moving to a new city or state can also be unsettling to your sense of confidence. As life brings significant change to you, it ushers away the familiar and manageable circumstances in which you built your confidence. The rug gets pulled out from under your feet, so to speak.

Some misguided risk-avoiders believe that if they just steer clear of change and risk in their lives, they can preserve their sense of self-confidence. What actually happens, however, is that their chronic unwillingness to change or take chances causes them to slowly fall behind – because, after all, life is changing all around them. When these stubborn individuals get into positions of leadership, they bring their teams to a screeching halt. They do everything they can to slow change and progress. They say no to good ideas. They get in the way. They refuse to make decisions on matters that will expose them and their teams to creativity. And, strangely, many seem to take great pride in exerting their power to stop progress in its tracks. Don't become this person, whatever you do. You will regret it, and so will the team relying on you.

Among the more serious challenges facing forensic scientists when it comes to earning and maintaining their professional confidence is avoiding the jadedness that can arise from being exposed to the adversarialism and cynicism that are endemic to today's criminal justice culture. In my experience, some people handle this very well, while others seem to crumble under the weight of the resulting emotional burdens. I think I probably fell somewhere in between. I tend to be an agreeable and caring guy who thrives off of personal connection. I often found the attitudes of some prosecutors and police officials to be nothing short of nasty. As a forensic scientist, you are in the position of having to interact professionally with criminal justice officials who are often tired, moody, combative, caustic, and demanding. Especially if you make a substantive mistake in your work, it can cultivate an environment where the loss of one's confidence is an occupational hazard.

If you ever find yourself in a position where you've lost some or all of your confidence, it is likely because you feel that you don't have the skills you need to meet your current responsibilities. Maybe you're struggling with some aspect of your work. Maybe you made a serious error. The good news is that you can earn back your confidence the same way you gained it in the first place, which is to rifle through the natural cycles of trying, failing, and succeeding. Those individuals who struggle to earn back their confidence often get snagged on their own egos. They just can't bring themselves to fail, so they don't try as hard as they must. Because they don't try, they never set into motion the self-developmental processes that lead to the earning of confidence. Isn't that interesting? You have to be willing to *fail* in order to earn your confidence!

So, here's what you need to do. First, you have to be honest and candid with the people around you. Make it clear that you are struggling a bit and that you might need some help from time to time. You don't need to lay this on too thick, just be clear that you've got a lot of work and learning to do to get to where you want to be. This is a critical step because our refusal to fail often stems from our desire to impress people. You might be surprised how motivated your colleagues will be to support you once you've made yourself vulnerable. Genuineness is very attractive and endearing. The assistance and encouragement you receive because of it will accelerate the growth of your confidence.

Second, sit down with a notebook and write out your strengths and weaknesses. What new or increased strengths will help you drive progress toward your goals? What weaknesses do you now have the motivation to correct? Your loss of confidence should inspire you to want to improve. What are those improvements? Be specific. There's no use in acting like you are confident when you are not. Not only will those around you see you as a fraud, you will see yourself as a fraud. And guess what that will do? Yep - it will further erode your confidence.

This is probably a good time for me to let you in on a little secret that professional coaches like me exploit to help our clients. We generally understand that, no matter what a client may be trying to achieve or correct in their careers, the one thing they desperately want is more confidence. As a coach, therefore, I focus on encouraging and enabling my clients to do the things that are necessary to *earn* that confidence. One of those things is coming to a clear understanding of one's strengths and weakness and how those strengths and weaknesses are manifesting themselves in all aspects of the client's life. Human beings have a remarkable capacity to only believe the things that are easy or more enjoyable to believe. As human beings, if we don't like a particular fact or if it makes us feel insecure, guilty, or ashamed, we can become obstinate and simply refuse to acknowledge it. Given enough time, however, this obstinance will begin to precipitate failures, some of which may be imperceptible at first. But eventually, one's refusal to embrace reality leads to a string of sizable failures or lost opportunities that erode his confidence.

Although this may seem counterintuitive, if you're looking to build or restore your confidence as quickly as possible, there's a few things you can do to accelerate the process. First, take a moment to pause and reflect on the moment at hand. Be thankful for your desire to improve and allow your psyche to be flooded with gratitude for the good things that are going to start happening for you in the near future. Your desire to improve is something that not everyone experiences. Be glad for it. Second, create a schedule. Pick a date in the future at which you believe you can achieve a strong sense of self-confidence. This won't happen on its own; there are things you need to do – very specific things. What are they? Third, atone for any damage you caused or mistakes you made that adversely affected other people or caused them to lose confidence in you. Make it clear to them that you have been struggling and are actively working to improve. Finally, carry out your plan. If you've designed it thoughtfully, it will indeed help you earn the confidence you are seeking.

Of course, it is worth reiterating that if your sense of self-awareness is low, or if you are in a state of self-denial that prevents you from accurately assessing your own strengths and weaknesses with sufficient clarity, it is likely that whatever plan you design will have significant flaws. Take whatever time you need to really think through all of the reasons why your confidence has been shaken, then resolve yourself to act on it to the best of your ability. That's how you begin to get your confidence back.

# PART 3

Expert Witnessing

# 30

## Courtroom Anxiety

No matter how many times I testify as an expert witness, I always find myself struggling to calm my nerves a bit. It does get easier the more times you do it, but in some ways it gets harder. Why? Because the more times you do it the higher the expectations placed upon you become. For me, it always seems like the butterflies in my stomach start fluttering when I get within a few miles of the courthouse. From there, the feeling of nervousness builds as the moment of truth nears.

What I'd like to do is share with you some tips I've learned and practiced over the years that have helped me to stay calm and effective in my courtroom testimony experiences. My hope is that you can use these as a foundation upon which to build your own approach to managing the normal stress and anxiety you will feel in your career as an expert witness.

This first one will sound familiar because I mentioned it previously in this book, albeit in the slightly different context of public speaking. It is also the most powerful, which is to adopt a *servant's mindset*. Let me take a moment to explain.

The primary source of an expert witness's anxiety is the prospect of being judged. This is because the expert, as most experts do, makes the mistake of adopting a *performer's mindset* in which she sees herself as putting on a show, a show that will be judged by others whose judgement actually matters. The performer's mindset is anxiety-provoking because it brings the possibility of failure onto the expert's plane of focus. The expert sees herself as a performer whose performance will either succeed, fail, or fall somewhere in between. Making matters worse, the judgement of whether the performance succeeds or fails is left to those in the courtroom who will hear the testimony. By adopting the performer's mindset, the expert witness unknowingly gives away her power and sense of self-security to people who probably don't even know her. Servants, on the other hand, are not people we typically *judge*. They are people we *appreciate*. With a servant's mindset, the expert witness does not burden herself with the demands placed on a performer. As a servant, she enters the courtroom not with the expectation of putting on a show or trying to impress people, but of trying to help.

Anxiety is a symptom of an unrealistic or unhealthy sense of self, not only in the enterprise of expert witnessing but in all aspects of life.

In addition to regulating your mindset, it is important to regulate the many physiological processes in the body that inflame anxiety. Deep breathing exercises are remarkably effective in calming your nerves. One particularly effective method is called *box breathing*. In box breathing, you take long slow inhales, hold your breath for a few seconds after your lungs fill to capacity, slowly exhale, then hold your breath for a few seconds after your lungs empty, then repeat over the course of 5 to 10 minutes. This exercise can produce an almost miraculous reduction in anxiety. So too can simply taking care of your body through healthy diet, exercise, and smart lifestyle choices. Healthy bodies living healthy lives are less vulnerable to the ravages of anxiety.

# 31

## Defending Your Science

My guess is that you regard yourself as a *scientist* who practices a *science*. In your capacity as an expert witness, the fact that you are a scientist and that you practice a science plays a significant role in the courts' determination of whether or not to admit your testimony, and how much weight to give that testimony if it is, in fact, admitted. The courts take official notice of the fact that you call yourself a scientist and that you say you practice a science. This gives you and your testimony more credibility, much more so than a farmer, for example, would have when testifying about what time of year a particular fertilizer is used to treat crops – say, if residues of that fertilizer were found on the body of a victim recovered from a river.

So then, let me ask you an easy question: *What is a science?* I dare you to look in a mirror right now and try to clearly articulate an answer. Can you? If you can, you are probably in the minority. If you can't, then why not? Any reasonable person would expect a scientist to know what a science is and to be able to explain it without a pregnant pause. Yet in my professional development workshops, I've made a practice of asking fully trained forensic scientists to tell me what a science is. Most can't. Some are so shocked by the question that they won't even try. Those that do try often butcher the answer so awfully that they sound amateurish.

If a party at trial wants to weaken your credibility or lessen the weight of your testimony, it can do so by portraying you as someone who claims to be a scientist but is not. It is vitally important that you be well-read and well-prepared to engage effectively in a conversation about relevant scientific matters and about science in general. Unfortunately, many laboratories are in such dire need to get new scientists trained and authorized to work cases that they spend very little time teaching new scientists about scientific basics. This developmental neglect comes to rear its ugly head when the scientist must endure a vigorous cross examination.

There is something else to keep in mind as well. Forensic science as an occupation generally struggles to command respect as a conglomerate of legitimate natural sciences, mainly because its origins appear rooted in policing, not in academia or research. As a forensic scientist, you are the voice of your profession. Not only are you tasked with the responsibility of being a competent scientist and expert witness, you are expected to be an ambassador for the entire profession. Being able to accurately and reliably defend the scientific bases of your conclusions is a core competency that cannot be abdicated under any circumstance. This, of course, requires you to understand and explain why your expert conclusions do, in fact, have a strong scientific basis – often to an audience that includes parties at trial who are suspicious of you and the work you do.

First, let's be crystal clear. The forensic disciplines practiced in crime laboratories are, in fact, scientific and rooted in science. The reason why they've earned the distinction of being scientific is because they were developed under controlled conditions over lengthy periods of time, which allowed their efficacy to be tested, monitored, and understood by a variety of independent individuals. Through practice, innovation, and experimentation, today's forensic laboratory disciplines are now well understood because we know how the tests performed within these disciplines behave under a variety of conditions. We know the types of questions they can answer. We know under what circumstances a test might fail or be misinterpreted. We understand and respect their capabilities just as we understand and respect their limitations. We know what qualifications a person must have to practice in these disciplines. And, we know what kinds of facilities, equipment, supplies, and procedures are needed to practice these disciplines reliably.

Science can be defined as a controlled and systematic way of gathering and processing information for the purpose of answering questions or solving problems in our world, where those who are dependent on science's answers and solutions have been reasonably protected from and made aware of the associated risks. It is an institution that makes human endeavors trustworthy. As powerful as science is, it is actually not that complicated. Those who intentionally adopt a very restrictive or narrow definition of science usually do so, in my opinion, because they want to eliminate from consideration a scientific practice that somehow stands in their way. This, of course, is irresponsible behavior, but it does not change what is actually the true definition of science. More important, the value of a scientific practice, or any practice for that matter, lies securely in the willingness of stakeholders to trust it.

In 2009, the National Academy of Sciences, through the National Research Council, published what became one of the most controversial documents in the history of forensic science. *Strengthening Forensic Science in the United States – A Path Forward* is a report that every forensic scientist should read. It was highly critical of the most commonly practiced forensic disciplines, bringing to question their scientific underpinnings. To its credit, the National Academy of Sciences was seeking to identify ways in which to strengthen forensic science, as the title of its report suggests. In many ways, it succeeded. But, in my view, the report missed its mark by basing its criticisms on an inappropriately narrow interpretation of what it means for something to be *scientific*.

Interestingly, during that same year, the National Academy of Sciences released the 3rd edition of a publication titled *On Being a Scientist – A Guide to Responsible Conduct in Research*. It is a level-headed, insightful perspective on what it means to be a scientist. Below is an excerpt I wish to bring to your attention:

*The scientific enterprise is built on a foundation of trust. Society trusts that scientific research results are an honest and accurate reflection of a researcher's work. Researchers equally trust that their colleagues have gathered data carefully, have used appropriate analytic and statistical techniques, have reported their results accurately, and have treated the work of other researchers with respect. When this trust is misplaced and the professional standards of science are violated, researchers are not just personally affronted - they feel that the base of their profession has been undermined. This would impact the relationship between science and society.*

In presenting this excerpt, I wish to reinforce that the scientific strength in what you do is founded upon the trust that you, your colleagues, your customers, and your many stakeholders have in it. If you practice a discipline within an accredited forensic science laboratory, your discipline is based in science. Whether or not it is *a science* is up for some debate because many science theorists view science as being strictly research, but this shouldn't matter for our purposes here. The ultimate question to be answered is *Can your work be trusted, and why?* It could take you a lifetime to learn all the ways that this question can be answered, so you might as well start now.

# 32

## Silenced in the Courtroom

Few things are more frustrating than having something important to say and not being allowed to say it. As an expert witness, I cannot tell you the number of times I've sat on the witness stand with knowledge relevant to the discussion at hand, but never being asked the question that would allow me to share that knowledge in open court. There have also been times when I decided to be bold and inject my knowledge or opinion without being asked, only to elicit an objection or be admonished by the judge or opposing counsel. *Just answer the questions, Mr. Collins* is a phrase I've heard more than a few times in my career.

    To a forensic scientist like you and me, the customs, rules, and practices of the courts sometimes seem nothing short of ridiculous. A criminal trial, I've come to believe after many years in this profession, is not a search for the truth; it is a *contest* in which there will be a winner and a loser. Yes, we have faith that the greater *macro-truth* about the defendant's guilt or innocence will emerge. But the many micro-truths that are relevant in criminal litigation are held like playing cards in a poker tournament. It is these micro-truths with which expert witnesses concern themselves. And, when those cards are not played in the sequence or manner that an expert believes is warranted, he becomes frustrated by what he perceives as gamesmanship and a lack of respect for the assistance he could offer the court if it would only allow it.

As an expert witness, your job is to answer questions - nothing more, nothing less. There will be times when you feel silenced or that you are not being used to the fullest extent possible by one party or another. But as an expert witness you probably do not know enough about the case to make that judgement. By the time a case goes to trial, there has been so much work done by the prosecution and defense that it is impossible for most expert witnesses to have any clue about what is actually relevant or irrelevant. This is especially true for forensic scientists working in public crime laboratories, experts who generally do not spend much time assisting prosecutors or defenders in trial preparation. You are too busy working all of the other cases flowing into your laboratory.

I must admit that I have felt that dreaded sense of entitlement and self-righteousness when being proclaimed an expert witness in court. It can make you feel as if you are the only one that has the secret map to the treasure everyone is looking for, and you expect to be granted the deference and respect owed to such an important person. This, of course, is not what expert witnessing is about. As an expert witness, you are a servant (as I explained earlier in this book). When you take the stand, you have no idea what is going on, what questions you will be asked, or what elements of the case each party is attempting to prove or disprove. Your frustrations will be assuaged if you simply relax, be attentive and professional, and just answer the questions that are asked of you. If you feel that an answer you gave has created confusion, the court will usually appreciate your effort to clarify your previous comments. But, whatever you do, do not make assumptions or judgements about what questions you believe the litigators should be asking or not asking. If you do, you will unnecessarily subject yourself to frustration, which may manifest itself in behaviors or body language that damage the court's regard for your skills and expertise.

# 33

## Conclusion Dismissed as *Just* Your Opinion

As a forensic firearms examiner, I often testified that I had conclusively identified a bullet as being fired from a specific firearm. Other forensic scientists, depending on their particular areas of expertise, give different kinds of answers to different kinds of questions, all of which are critical to establishing the elements of proof or disproof at trial. A reasonable follow-up question often asked by opposing counsel is, *This is just your opinion, correct*? The goal here is to take some of the steam out of the expert witness's scientific conclusion by dismissing it as simply an opinion and not a divine declaration of indisputable fact.

It is here that I wish to broach a theme that will underlie subsequent sections of this book, which is the danger of scientists, in their role as expert witnesses, being tricked or manipulated into using legal terminology. *Opinion*, it must be recognized, is a legal term used to describe courtroom testimony that does not represent the witness's direct knowledge or observation. An opinion is a personal interpretation. Testifying that *the apple was red*, is as statement of fact. Testifying that *the fruit was red, therefore it was likely an apple* is an opinion.

*Opinion*, however, is not a scientific term. Science is not in the business of producing opinions, thank goodness. In science, properly trained professionals conduct analyses that adhere to proper methods, which result in a scientific determination, result, or conclusion. In the general population, anyone can have an opinion about anything. But it doesn't work this way in science.

It is completely appropriate, in my view, to remind the court during expert testimony that the word *opinion* is a legal term and not one generally used in science. Instead, what you are presenting to the court is actually a carefully prepared scientific *determination*.

Consider the following line of questioning:

**Attorney**: *Ms. Sampson, would you please restate for the court what your opinion was in the case?*

**Expert**: *I concluded that the bullet recovered from autopsy, marked as People's Exhibit #12, was fired from the firearm marked as People's Exhibit #2.*

**Attorney**: *Now, this is just your opinion correct? You could be wrong, isn't that true?*

**Expert**: *The answer to your first question, sir, is that 'opinion' is a legal term and I am not a lawyer. I'm reporting to the court a scientific determination made based on direct observation, adherence to standard methods, and the application of strict quality assurance measures. The answer to your second question is, yes. Because I'm a human being, everything I do has the potential for error. Science exists to minimize that error, which is why I try to be responsible about the terminology I use when testifying in court.*

As a forensic scientist, stay true to your scientific foundations because it's safer there. Your conclusions may be opinions in a legal sense, but they are much more than that in the world of science. Be prepared to address that distinction when it becomes necessary.

# 34

## Answering Leading Questions

Trial attorneys live by a principle that is universally accepted in the practice law – *never ask a question to which you don't know the answer*. Questions are not asked of expert witnesses in court because a trial attorney is curious about the answer. Questions are asked to elicit a desired answer. It is the job of the trial attorney to build an argument, and this requires that specific elements be established and proved to the satisfaction of the judge or jury. As an expert witness, you are able to give answers that allow these elements to be established. That is why you were called to testify.

In the heat of courtroom battle, attorneys will both intentionally and unintentionally lead their witnesses in ways that assure specific answers are given at the right times. This can actually have a beneficial impact as it helps to guide laypersons who might otherwise be inappropriately abrupt or verbose. But for expert witnesses who are bound by professional and ethical standards of conduct, leading questions are to be handled with the utmost caution. Under no circumstance should a forensic scientist allow herself to be led into giving an answer that is not scientifically justified.

Often, leading questions are confronted with an objection by opposing counsel. If sustained, this will prompt a call by the judge to rephrase the question or ask a different question. But, as I've experienced in my own career, the judge and trial attorneys are rather lenient when it comes to leading questions during expert testimony. It's as if there is an understanding that the witness is a professional and can take care of herself. Moreover, the judge and attorneys know that the expert witness is bound by standards of professionalism and is unlikely to give an answer that is a surprise or is in conflict with the evidence. This means that it's up to each and every expert witness to pay close attention to the questions being asked and protect against being tricked into giving an answer the expert might later regret.

When faced with a leading question, the easiest thing to do is ask that it be rephrased; and be willing to explain that you are unable to answer the question as it was asked. Another tactic – one that I employ more often than not – is to answer the question that *should* have been asked. This is not an act of deception or manipulation but rather an attempt to economize your testimony by helping out the questioning attorney.

In more serious instances where you feel forced to answer a question that you feel is problematic, it is within your rights as a witness to ask the judge directly for some assistance. Some judges are more accommodating of this approach than others and can even depend on what mood they are in or how they feel about the attorney who subpoenaed you. I would recommend using this approach as a very last resort because it can make you appear uneasy or combative, but it is an option that you can consider if you feel it becomes necessary.

In giving your expert testimony, listen carefully to each and every question and be mindful of the answers you are giving. It is your job to answer questions, but it is also your job to avoid misleading the court.

# 35

## Courtroom Admonishment

While testifying in a murder trial in Decatur, Georgia many years ago, I was asked how semi-automatic pistols work. After being handed the actual murder weapon by the prosecutor, I began to explain. I pointed out where ammunition is loaded and demonstrated how the slide is pulled back against very strong spring tension and locked into place. Then came time for me to depress the slide release, as I had done in court many times before - causing the mainspring to drive the slide forward, stripping an unfired cartridge from the magazine and pushing it securely into the chamber. This would complete my task of explaining to the jury how a shooter would load the gun and prepare to fire it.

What I did not realize was that the witness stands in the DeKalb County Courthouse were not outfitted with the typical stem-mounted microphones that I could bring close to my mouth as I usually did to make myself easier to hear. Instead, the microphone was flat and mounted directly to the work surface in front of me. When I released the slide of the gun, which was directly above the microphone, the sound was amplified so much that it sounded as if the gun discharged. All 12 jurors jumped in their seats, as did the prosecutors, defense team, the judge, and the court reporter. In shocked embarrassment, I glanced toward the judge who was now leaning toward me and removing his reading glasses. "Mr. Collins," the judge warned, "if you ever do that in my courtroom again it will be the last time you testify here."

I apologized profusely to the jury, the judge, and everyone else in the courtroom, at least those who didn't need to make an emergency run to the restrooms. For the next hour or so, I continued my testimony, but it seemed to ring hollow. I felt like a small child with chocolate smeared on his face trying to tell his parents that he didn't sneak a bite of dad's birthday cake. At that moment, I felt like I had lost the respect of the jury – whether it was true or not.

If you testify enough times, you will eventually encounter a situation where the judge admonishes you for some reason. It may be something you did or maybe not. It may be entirely deserved, as it was with me, or you might just be a victim of unexpected circumstances. Either way, it's no fun to be called out by a judge at trial, and it can throw you off your game if you let it. When it happens, just accept it, thank the judge, and tell her that you will be more careful in the future. Apologize if you know that you did something careless or unprofessional, but only if you know you did. Don't apologize simply to gain favor with the court because it may be interpreted as an admission of something you didn't actually do. Never - and I mean never! - argue with a judge in court. This is a mortal sin from which you may never recover. Make your peace with the judge as quickly as possible and return your attention to the attorney who is conducting his witness examination.

If you are admonished in court for any reason, I'd like to strongly suggest that you advise your laboratory's director and quality manager as soon as possible. Explain to them what happened so that if they receive a call from the judge or other officer of the court, they will not be surprised by it and will already know your side of the story. They will also appreciate the courtesy you are showing to them.

# 36

## Prosecutorial Bias

The percentage of time that forensic scientists from publicly funded crime laboratories are called to testify by the prosecution is probably in excess of 95%. Very rarely are they called by the defense, which creates the unfortunate appearance that forensic science is a biased enterprise. During cross examination, it is common for defense attorneys to ask forensic scientists how often they testify for the defense knowing that jurors may be surprised to learn how infrequent it is. It is a legitimate line of questioning, but forensic scientists should know how to address the criticisms that can arise in its wake.

We should first note that ethical and honorable expert witnesses do not testify *for* or *against* any of the competing parties in a criminal trial. Expert witnesses may be *called* by the prosecution or defense, but their testimony is for everyone in the courtroom. And, quite candidly, experts appearing to favor one side or the other come across to judges and juries as being slick and seedy. Some professional experts in private practice don't really care. They get paid just the same. But for forensic scientists paid for by taxpayer dollars, this is unacceptable.

Now back to prosecutorial bias, specifically. That forensic scientists are called so frequently by the prosecution is, of course, not because of bias. It is because prosecutors are the only parties in criminal litigation who are required to prove anything. A defendant on trial for a crime, on the other hand, has no burden of proof. If he so chooses, he can opt not to call a single witness or ask a single question. The prosecution does not have this option. In representing the people, it must present its case.

Also, police who investigate crimes, with very few exceptions, do their jobs very well. The people they arrest and charge with the commission of crimes are actually the people who committed those crimes – again, with very few exceptions. Consequently, the physical evidence associated with those crimes will tend to incriminate the defendant, which is why prosecutors need it to be presented in court. The people best able to do this are forensic scientists like you and me.

This explanation of the relationship between prosecutors and forensic scientists shows there is no inherent bias in the forensic science enterprise in favor of prosecutors. It does not mean, however, that *individual* forensic scientists can't or won't develop inappropriate biases of their own. When you find yourself working so often with prosecutors, you are vulnerable to developing unhealthy loyalties to them and their cause. Having good cordial working relationships with prosecutors is entirely acceptable as long as it does not evolve into a sense of obligation that erodes your professional objectivity in court.

Some of the most professional and enjoyable people I've ever worked with in my career were prosecutors. The vast majority of them want and expect their expert witnesses to be objective and professional no matter what. They don't want to convict defendants based on slanted or exaggerated evidence. So, if a forensic scientist develops a sense of loyalty to the prosecution, it won't be because of the prosecution. It will be because of a personal bias that requires attention and correction.

The best thing you as a forensic scientist can do is simply be aware of the issues related to prosecutorial bias so that you can explain it, avoid it, and recognize any temptation to be consumed by it.

# 37

## Sympathy for the Defendant

Over the course of my career, I've had several opportunities to conduct private work for the defense. In doing so, I discovered that I was far more vulnerable to developing a sense of favoritism for a defendant than I ever was for the prosecution. I think there's a couple reasons for this. First, the defendants who hired me did so at their own expense, which means they were my clients - and there's a natural desire to want to deliver value to those who place their trust and financial resources in you. Second, defendants in criminal litigation are the underdogs. They are going up against the full prosecutorial power of the government, which makes them sympathetic figures, especially if the crimes for which they've been charged have mitigating factors. If you happen to be a forensic scientist working in private practice, you can probably appreciate some of the things I'm talking about here.

If you are a forensic scientist working in a publicly funded laboratory, one who's usually called by the prosecution, you can still find yourself experiencing sympathy for the defendant in certain situations. Many criminal defendants are poor and have suffered difficult life experiences. Some are mentally or emotionally unbalanced. In some situations, as I've experienced to my dismay, defendants are overcharged by aggressive prosecutors or there is very little evidence supporting a conviction.

One case in particular was among the most egregious examples of prosecutorial misconduct I've ever witnessed. I was hired by the defense team of a famous professional basketball player who was charged with criminal sexual assault. Although there was a sexual encounter with a female who later claimed to have been raped, the complainant's story changed several times during the investigation and there was absolutely no physical evidence that a rape occurred. He was eventually acquitted. But I recall the emotional effort I had to make to prevent myself from being influenced by my strong belief that he was factually innocent of the crime for which he was prosecuted.

As I've explained earlier, expert witnesses do not have access to all relevant information in a criminal proceeding. It is not the job of the expert to advocate for a particular judicial outcome. It is the job of the expert witness to help the court understand the evidence.

The responsibilities of expert witnesses are formally codified in what are known as the Federal Rules of Evidence. Rule 702 specifically addresses expert opinions and provides a clear framework for how expert witnesses are to be used in courts of law. I will close this section by presenting Federal Rule of Evidence 702 on Testimony by Expert Witnesses:

*A witness who is qualified as an expert by knowledge, skill, experience, training, or education may testify in the form of an opinion or otherwise if:*

*(a) the expert's scientific, technical, or other specialized knowledge will help the trier of fact to understand the evidence or to determine a fact in issue;*

*(b) the testimony is based on sufficient facts or data;*

*(c) the testimony is the product of reliable principles and methods; and*

*(d) the expert has reliably applied the principles and methods to the facts of the case.*

# 38

## Expressing Your Scientific Certainty

*Just so the jury understands your testimony today, is it true that this is your conclusion to a reasonable degree of scientific certainty?*

If you haven't before been asked this question in court, you probably will. The purpose of the question is to assess the degree of confidence you have in your conclusions, but to do so within a framework of legal judgement. *Reasonable degree of scientific certainty* is a legal standard, not a scientific one. When the above question is posed to you, you are basically being asked to assume the role of lawyer, not the role of a scientist. Therefore, you are well advised not to indulge.

True scientists do not concern themselves with degrees of certainty. In science, we focus on *confidence* – the confidence a scientist has in the quality of the work he did and the accuracy of any conclusions he drew. This is not to suggest that a scientist's confidence must be expressed as a numerical value such as, *I am 95% confident*. This would be an unethical assertion to share in a court of law if there was no reliable scientific or statistical basis upon which to do so. In my experience, confidence is best evaluated through conversation, where the scientist can explain why he believes his work is accurate, what the most likely causes of error are in this type of work, and how those likely causes of error were mitigated in the work done in *this* case.

Herein lies a glaring weakness in how our courts search for the truth. Courts to do not permit conversation, which is actually the best way to evaluate the quality of scientific work. Forcing experts to answer questions, while affording them little latitude to expand on their answers, is a rather poor way of evaluating the reliability of scientific evidence. But, as we all know, that's the way the system works, and it's our job as forensic science professionals to work within the system as it is.

Let me share an example of what expert testimony might sound like after an expert is asked whether or not his conclusions are accurate to a reasonable degree of scientific certainty:

*Thank you for the question, but I should mention that the term 'reasonable degree of scientific certainty' is a legal standard and not one we use in science. In science we focus on confidence, and my testimony today is that I am confident that the work I did in this case and the conclusions I am reporting today are reliable. I have no reason to believe that any mistakes were made, or that I am making any mistakes now in my testimony. In science, however, there is always a potential for error and it's my job to be prepared to talk about it and how these potential sources of error are mitigated – and I am certainly happy to do that. That being said, I have no reason to doubt the accuracy or reliability of the work I did in this case.*

The above answer, of course, is in narrative form, which may or may not be allowed depending on the context of the question. But because the questioner likely wants the judge or jury to hear how confident you are, you will likely be given the latitude to elaborate on the subject of confidence. But, again, the point here is to ensure that as science professionals we not allow ourselves to be pigeonholed into using terminology that we're not trained or qualified to use.

# 39

## Feeling Joy or Sadness About a Verdict

Every now and then, prosecutors or defenders will call to tell me what the final verdict was in cases in which I testified. The motive, of course, is to share their joy or disappointment with me, believing that I will share in that joy or disappointment because I was "playing on their team."

I will be the first to admit that when I am called to testify by the prosecution and I learn that there was a conviction, there is a part of me that feels some sense of satisfaction. And, trust me, I think I am probably about as objective and dispassionate an expert witness as one can be. But it has always bothered me – and it still does - that I would feel any personal emotions about a verdict. At the same time, when called as an expert for the defense, I have felt the same sense of satisfaction when learning of an acquittal.

A hawkish reader might take issue with my admissions here, and they would be justified in doing so. Expert witnesses who are ethical and honorable care about giving a voice to the evidence, not seeking a particular judicial outcome. Well, that of course is true, but I think there is more to the emotional experience of being an expert witness that needs to be understood and appreciated.

First, when you work with trial attorneys you develop an appreciation for them as you get to know them a little bit, if you don't already. So, when a verdict comes down that elates or disappoints them, you may feel emotions that are actually more associated with your sense of empathy than your feelings about the verdict itself. There is nothing wrong with empathy; in fact, it is among the most powerful and useful of human capabilities – the ability to see a situation from someone else's viewpoint.

On the other hand, there are times when a forensic scientist becomes closely involved in an investigation during the early phase. This usually happens because the scientist's subject-matter expertise is especially relevant. Over time, however, this highly engaged forensic scientist may develop an opinion about the guilt or innocence of the defendant once the case goes to trial. This, of course, can be dangerous if the expert allows her feelings to erode her professional objectivity. The final verdict may then spark intense feelings of accomplishment or failure, which is a sign that she allowed herself to become more personally vested in the matter than was appropriate. This does not mean she is incapable of giving accurate and reliable testimony. But it does mean that she has exposed herself and the court to greater risk.

To put it succinctly, there's nothing wrong with a forensic scientist feeling emotions about a verdict. But they may signal an unhealthy sense of personal obligation to certain parties in certain cases. Expert witnesses are human beings and always will be. It is their humanity that makes them reliable and trustworthy, so we want that humanity to shine through. But it's also our humanity that makes us and our work vulnerable to malpractice. I therefore encourage all forensic scientists, prior to testifying in court, to remind themselves that they have no official opinion about the guilt or innocence of the defendant, and do not have access to all the information necessary to have such an opinion. This sets the stage for more objective and professional testimony.

# 40

## Distrusted Due to Police Affiliations

The overwhelming majority of forensic scientists working in publicly funded laboratories fall under the control and authority of a chief of police, sheriff, or other law enforcement administrator. Among them, most work in a state law enforcement agency, such as a department of state police, state bureau of investigation, or department of public safety. This close affiliation of forensic science with law enforcement has been in place for well over a century and will probably not change anytime soon despite the increasing attention being paid to the nature of this relationship, its advantages, and disadvantages.

Coincidentally, this book is being written several weeks after the death of George Floyd in Minneapolis, which sparked an eruption of civil rights protests and demands for more racially sensitive policing strategies. To be blunt, this is not a fun time to be a uniformed police officer in many cities, and the reputation of the policing profession has never been subjected to such strong and unified criticisms. It is my hope that the policing profession will improve dramatically in the coming years, as it has done in years past, and I hope these improvements come to benefit the profession of forensic science as well.

Among the most challenging criticisms forensic scientists face is that their close affiliation with law enforcement biases them in favor of the prosecution, or perhaps exposes them to undue pressures from police commanders who insist on having their investigative hunches validated by their forensic staff. There are a lot of arguments that can be made questioning the trustworthiness of forensic scientists working in police agencies, but there are four key points that all forensic scientists should understand and be able to articulate when confronted by this criticism:

1. **Accreditation** – The accreditation of forensic science laboratories has dramatically improved the organizational cultures of forensic science laboratories, and it has forced police commanders to respect the cultural independence that forensic science laboratories need to remain credible and trustworthy.

2. **Educational Credentials** – Unlike years past, forensic scientists today require academic degrees, many of which are heavily weighted in science. It is no longer acceptable for a high school graduate to go through a police academy, patrol the roads for a couple years, then transfer into a forensic laboratory.

3. **Civilian Workforce** – Over the last 30 years, there has been a remarkable transition of forensic science laboratories from having sworn police officers or state troopers in scientist positions to, in most cases, an entirely civilian workforce.

4. **Operational Separation** – With the proliferation of accreditation, the security of forensic science laboratories has tightened considerably. Laboratories have advanced intrusion-prevention systems that prevent non-laboratory personnel from accessing areas where evidence is tested and stored.

# 41

## Believing Strongly that the Defendant is Guilty

In a previous section, I briefly mentioned the potential of an expert witness to become vested in a judicial outcome. For forensic scientists, the risk of this happening is greater when they are intimately involved in an investigation. This is not to suggest that I support the recommendations of some critics who argue that forensic scientists should be kept *blind*, having little or no knowledge of the details of an investigation. I flatly reject this mainly because it robs forensic scientists of their sense of professional relevance, which will make it harder to attract and retain top talent in the future. The result would be a deteriorating workforce and more errors. But it is important for forensic scientists to know how to manage biases or prejudices with professionalism.

If you ever find yourself in a situation where you feel strongly that the defendant is guilty, it is not necessary to recuse yourself and you should not feel bad about yourself. But you should recognize that you are at risk and must take steps to mitigate that risk so that you and the defendant are not harmed.

The most important thing you can do in this situation is to ask yourself some important questions:

- *What if the defendant is really innocent?*
- *What if my opinions about this case are being distorted by factors that fall outside my awareness?*
- *What if this is an outlier case in which a 'perfect storm' of factors are conspiring to incriminate an innocent person?*
- *What if there is prosecutorial misconduct happening?*
- *What if the defense attorney is incompetent and failing to give his client his best effort?*

The purpose of asking yourself these questions is that it sharpens your alertness to things you might otherwise miss. As a forensic scientist, you are often looking at things for the first time, analyzing evidence that has never been analyzed before. A strong belief in the suspect's guilt will make it less likely that you will notice something suggestive of the suspect's innocence. Conversely, if you've seriously considered the possibility that a prime suspect in a case may be innocent, your senses will be heightened, and you will be more likely to see something or think of something that's indicative of innocence.

As a forensic scientist, you will always perform better and more reliably when you choose to believe *nothing* about a suspect's or defendant's guilt or innocence. Remind yourself that it's not even your job to make such a determination. Instead, it is your job to answer questions, to compare things and analyze things, and to answer the questions asked of you inside and outside of the courtroom. The fact that you may feel a strong sense that the defendant is factually guilty does not mean that you cannot quickly recalibrate your thinking by asking yourself the questions I posed to you above. And remember, the next case you work could be the case that shocks you to your core.

# 42

## Believing Strongly that the Defendant is Innocent

Few things are more disturbing to criminal justice officials than the possibility of convicting and sentencing an innocent defendant. Criminal justice, for all its challenges and weaknesses, is an enterprise that does quite well considering the volume of cases that must be managed each and every day. With very few exceptions, prosecutors work diligently to ensure that innocent people are not charged for crimes they did not commit. If someone is to be prosecuted, it is because there is sufficient evidence to justify it.

As an expert witness who's worked in private practice, I've chosen to involve myself in cases where I believed the defendant was either innocent or had been overcharged. Overcharging, in my opinion, is a common occurrence, but tends to be open to legal interpretation. As expert witnesses, we aren't typically in a position to have an official opinion about guilt or innocence. But, from time to time, there are those cases where it seems like something is wrong. You may not be able to put your finger on it, but you just know. The best thing to do is simply share your concerns with a member of the prosecution team. Chances are that your concerns will be alleviated. But if they're not, what do you do? What if you believe strongly that there is a potential for a grave miscarriage of justice?

The chance of this happening, in my opinion, is remote at best. But if it *does* happen, I'd like you to be prepared for it. If you are employed as a forensic scientist by an organization such as a police agency or private laboratory, whatever you decide to do, you are acting as an official representative of your employer, so it will be necessary for you to involve your employer. If you are self-employed, you have more flexibility to express your concerns to anyone who will listen, even it if means compromising any existing working relationships you may have with the prosecution team.

If you are like most forensic scientists working in a public agency, it is my recommendation that the head of your agency or her delegate request a formal meeting with the prosecution and defense to discuss what's going on. But under no circumstance should you or your agency express a formal opinion about guilt or innocence; that is the prosecutor's job. Instead, your concerns about the defendant's possible innocence must be based on the evidence. Simply explain what it is about the evidence you find to be exculpatory. In doing so, a couple things may happen. First, the prosecution may lower the charges or drop them entirely. Second, the defense may subpoena you to testify as a witness, so you will have a chance to express your concerns in court. Third, the head of your agency may feel compelled to address the matter at a higher level. This may include reaching out to the judge, your state's supreme court, court administrative office, or appellate defender's office.

Finally, in any serious judicial matter, don't hesitate to reach out to a constitutional law professor at one of your local or state universities. They will probably enjoy the opportunity to assist you and will likely have some helpful thoughts about what you should and should not do with the concerns you have. Prosecutors have tremendous power and authority that must be respected. But as a private citizen, you have power as well. Use it with caution.

# 43

## Helping Out the Court Reporter

The following is an excerpt from the National Court Reporters Association on the role and purpose of court reporters in the United States:

*Court reporters, also known as guardians of the record because of their impartiality and role within the judicial process, capture the words spoken by everyone during a court or deposition proceeding. Court reporters then prepare verbatim transcripts of proceedings. The official record or transcript helps safeguard the legal process. When litigants want to exercise their right to appeal, they will use the transcript to provide an accurate record of what transpired during their case. During the discovery phase, attorneys also use deposition transcripts to prepare for trial.*

Early in my career I was fortunate to gain an appreciation for how important court reporters are to the judicial process, and how important they are to expert witnesses whose spoken testimony is forever memorialized in court transcripts. When testifying as an expert witness, it's important to remain aware of the court reporter. Here is a list of a few things I do and think about to help make life a bit easier for court reporters.

Keep these in mind because you will also impress the judge with the respect you are showing the court:

- When I testify as an expert witness, I make a point to say hello to the court reporter as I am taking the stand.

- Before my testimony begins, I will pull the microphone up to my mouth, turn to the court reporter, and ask if he can hear me. Usually he will smile and say "yes, thank you."

- When I am asked to say and spell my name for the court, I sometimes look to the court reporter while I am doing it, reinforcing my desire to have may name spelled correctly in the transcript. Sometimes I look at the jury when saying and spelling my name, but this usually depends on where the court reporter is seated in the courtroom.

- When using highly technical words or jargon, I will often pause, look to the court reporter, and then spell the word for him. Court reporters love when experts do this because it saves them a lot of work trying to confirm the spelling of unusual words.

- When my testimony is over, I sometimes look to the court reporter, nod my head, and say thank you. This assumes the court reporter is looking at me, which they sometimes do, but sometimes don't.

When you were trained by your laboratory on being an effective expert witness, you may not have learned much about court reporters because they are not actually part of the question-and-answer exchanges that occur between witnesses and the attorneys. But if you want to really take your expert witnessing skills to the next level, be mindful of the court reporter and make whatever effort you can to acknowledge him and assist him as you testify. Your efforts will be truly appreciated!

# 44

## Court Orders and Judicial Pressures

Within the courtroom, it is usually the opposing attorneys who wage war. But, from time to time, the court will assert its power when it believes it has been wronged. To be found or held in *contempt of court* is known as a *process crime*, which means the court has found an individual or organization to have been disrespectful or disobedient. The punishment for such process crimes can be jail or fine. The ability to charge someone with contempt of court is among the highest powers a judge holds, used for the purpose of preserving the dignity, authority, efficiency, and responsibility of her court.

As a forensic scientist, both in your role as a scientist and as an expert witness, you have the potential to be held in contempt of court if it's determined that the needs or wishes of the court were violated in any way. As you might guess, it is very unusual for this to happen; but it *can* happen. Generally speaking, judges will not hold you in contempt of court if they see you are making a sincere effort to be responsive. But if the court regards your behavior as careless, unprofessional, or unbecoming of someone in your position, it will hold you in contempt if simply to teach you a lesson and ensure that it does not happen again.

Over the last 20 years as demand for forensic science services has skyrocketed, case backlogs have repeatedly delayed the cause of justice in many jurisdictions. Judges are smart enough to know this is not entirely the fault of the forensic scientists. They are also smart enough to know that a direct order from the court will speed up the process, forcing a laboratory to make the case a priority. If the laboratory, for whatever reason, does not comply with the order, the scientist along with his laboratory's director may be summoned to explain to the court why the work was not completed as ordered. If the court is sufficiently irritated, it may hold a *show cause hearing*, which is held to determine if a charge of contempt is warranted. If the circumstances are deemed appropriate, a forensic scientist, laboratory administrator, or both can be held in contempt and potentially fined or jailed.

Although some judges can be very pushy with regards to issuing court orders and demanding that forensic testing be completed within a prescribed period of time, those same judges often don't realize the pressures that forensic science laboratories are under. Worse – and I hate to even bring this up because of how egregious it is – I have personally witnessed prosecutors who dragged their feet in moving a case along unfairly blame their forensic laboratories for the delay. As the director of the Michigan laboratory system, I once confronted a prosecutor's office in Detroit that was blaming our laboratories for not completing forensic work on time for trial. The truth was that the evidence had never been submitted to our labs!

If you or your laboratory find yourself in hot water with a court or judge in a criminal case, don't panic. Usually the only thing needed to remedy the situation is an update to help the judge understand what's going on. But if it becomes a disruptive pattern, your laboratory may need to reach out to an administrator of the courts for assistance. Forensic laboratories can only do so much, and judges do not have the authority to issue orders for things that can't reasonably be delivered.

# 45

## Cynicism

So, as we close Part 3 of this book dealing with situations related to expert witnessing, let's agree to admit and accept that much about our criminal justice system is just plain weird. It's strange, disjointed, inflexible, political, adversarial, and downright inefficient. Never in a million years would we want our favorite sports teams, our children's schools, our churches, our local grocery stores, our doctor's offices, or the organizations in which we work to be managed the way our criminal justice system is. In fact, let me correct myself - our criminal justice system is *not* managed at all; it is held steady by opposing forces – much like a tall communications tower is kept from toppling by long anchoring cables.

As scientists, the chaos and gamesmanship of the criminal justice enterprise can seem offensive. So too can the strict micromanagement of communications within the courtroom, which seems to stifle the kinds of conversation and open debate that scientists value as being critical to any legitimate truth-seeking process. As forensic scientists, we've chosen a career that subjects us to this apparent nonsense with unrelenting frequency, resulting in feelings of cynicism that rob us of our job satisfaction if we allow it. For all its faults and inefficiencies, our criminal justice system succeeds far more often than it fails, so any cynicism we experience may be reasonable in the short term, but not as a chronic source of emotional toxicity.

As forensic scientists, it's our responsibility to leverage scientific expertise in assisting our courts, not to make our courts more scientific. There is and will always be inherent tensions whenever science and law comingle. Our success, therefore, will depend on our ability to accept the weaknesses and limitations of the criminal justice system, respect its strengths and capabilities, and do our best to help it make good use of the evidence before it. In many ways, forensic scientists are like translators facilitating communication in a foreign land. Physical evidence speaks a language of its own, and it is an honor to make it understandable to those who would otherwise ignore it.

If you find yourself coping with feelings of cynicism such that it erodes some of your joy and professional acuity, it is likely that your expectations of the criminal justice system are not entirely reasonable. It may also be that the expectations you have of yourself and the role you are attempting to play are unreasonable as well. Remember that our criminal justice system needs to be competent enough to administer justice to the guilty while being disorganized enough to be incapable of preying upon the innocent. Don't get me wrong here; there are lots of things about the American criminal justice system that I wish would change as quickly as possible. And although you may feel helpless in your inability to make it better, your professionalism and expertise are critically important to every judge, juror, victim, defendant, prosecutor, and defender you will encounter over the course of your career. By being the best you can be, you are playing a small but important part in the evolution of our criminal justice system as it transitions from what it is now to what it will someday become. In that knowledge, I hope you find great joy, satisfaction, and peace of mind.

# PART 4

Thinking About Your Future

# 46

## Considering a Management Position

As you think about the future of your career – and I'm sure you do – you probably realize that being promoted into a managerial position within your laboratory is usually the fastest way to increase your compensation without leaving your current employer and moving to another laboratory. Moving from a scientist position into a supervisory position allows you to jump into a new and higher job classification resulting in increased pay. With increased pay comes increased opportunities to save for retirement, buy or rent a nicer home, pay for your kids' college, or take more expensive vacations to more interesting places. With more pay, there are more options and that's why so many of us are eager to dip our toes into the management pool.

I encourage you wholeheartedly to take an interest in management, even if you aren't sure that it's right for you. But I want to add one point of clarification; do so long before you give it serious consideration as a career path. Promotional candidates who make the best first-time managers, in my experience, are those who gain a sincere appreciation for management and its responsibilities in a natural, organic way. They think about it. They imagine what they would do if they were in charge. They recognize their own skills and abilities and can envision themselves leveraging those skills and abilities for the good of the team. They are as intrigued by the potential challenges of management as they are its potential rewards. But most important, their ambition to become a manager is preceded by a genuine fascination with all that it entails.

A reliable indicator that you are not ready for a management position is that its attractiveness is based solely on its promise of higher compensation and the opportunity to gain power. If these are why management interests you, then you would be well-advised to wait a while before giving it a try. The cultural damage you could potentially cause your team, and the resulting hardships you will bring upon yourself, will negate just about any satisfaction that comes simply from being paid more or having more authority. Management is a form of service to a team of people who are counting on you to empower *them*. When you get to a point where you feel energized by the opportunity to make a positive impact on other people through leadership, then you know you are probably ready to take on the challenge.

Over many years, as a leader and executive coach, I've come to the unmistakable conclusion that young professionals are getting into management too early in their careers. They are taking on important leadership responsibilities without having the life experience needed to put the most complex and sensitive leadership issues into perspective. This, of course, is an entirely subjective interpretation of reality, but I believe it to be true. Ideally, I would like to see you take on your first management position no earlier than the age of 30. But if an attractive opportunity comes along earlier than that, then go after it. You can always find good leadership training and leadership coaching to help accelerate your development.

Finally, if you decide that management is not right for you, congratulations! You probably made one of the smartest decisions you will ever make. Perhaps you will feel differently about it in the future but, for now, just focus on being the best forensic scientist you can be.

# 47

## Becoming a First-Time Manager

Leadership is all about negotiating the challenges and opportunities that life brings to you and your team. It's not easy, but it doesn't have to be chronically difficult either. When things are going well, leadership is fun and satisfying. When things aren't going so well, it is mentally and emotionally taxing. Your goal, therefore, is to build and protect a culture that makes people want to come to work each day and volunteer their best efforts. If you are to accomplish this goal, you have to do the right things and avoid the wrong ones. So, I want to share a perspective on leadership that will help you get started as an effective manager – today.

When you were promoted into a position of management, you were not rewarded with anything. Yes, other people may have been interested in the position and didn't get it, but your promotion was not a *win*. Too many first-time managers make the mistake of thinking that their promotions were a celebration of greatness and a gesture of thanks for previous successes. This causes feelings of entitlement that are poisonous to effective leadership. Entitled leaders are failures in the making.

So, here's what actually happened when you were promoted. You were *entrusted* with the responsibility of caring for your team and enabling the greatness of its members. The decision was made that *you* are the person in whose hands the future of the team should rest. Nothing about this should inflate your ego or give you a feeling of power. That's what happens to entitled leaders, and that's not what we want for you. I want you to be an *entrusted* leader. This means that you feel a strong sense of purpose, responsibility, and accountability. You see yourself not as a boss but as a partner. You accept blame while generously giving credit. You listen far more often than you speak. You are more likely to ask good questions than give directions. If there is something members of your team can do for themselves, you give them the space to do it. You learn from your people more than you teach them. And, when your team finds itself dealing with serious adversity, you are a source and example of strength and focus under pressure. You are more than just a manager; you are a leader.

When I have the opportunity to coach new managers, I encourage them to see their employees as sources of learning and knowledge, not as people that need to be controlled or educated. This is perhaps the biggest mistake that new managers make – they treat their new authority like a toy that needs to be played with. In doing so, the new manager makes her leadership authority about her and not about the well-being of her team. When this happens, the team members can clearly see that she doesn't know how to use her new leadership authority responsibility, so they begin to resent and resist her.

The key to earning trust as a leader is to make it clear to everyone on your team that your top priority is the health, well-being, and effectiveness of every team member. You must appreciate and admire the good qualities that your team members have, and be a trusted partner in helping them recognize and improve any areas of weakness that may be getting in the way. You will be judged by how you make people feel, not by what you tell them to do. Make them feel empowered, responsible, trusted, and effective because that's what they'll become.

# 48

## Enjoying Your Career

The story goes like this. Two neighbors, Hal and Nick meet at the end of their driveways to go for a morning walk. They've been friends for many years, and this is their morning ritual. After exchanging greetings, they set out. Hal looks at Nick with a smile and says "It's such a beautiful morning! Perfect temperature and not a cloud in the sky!"

Nick rolls his eyes as if to be irritated by Hal's ignorance. "My friend," Nick replies, "that sky may look nice, but it's full of pollution, warmer than it should be thanks to climate change, and is probably going to kill millions of people if we humans don't change the way we live."

Still smiling, Hal turns to Nick with an almost sympathetic glare. "You know, Nick, nothing you just said changes what I appreciate about that beautiful sky up there. As long as there is something to enjoy, I choose to enjoy it. When I'm *not* enjoying it, I'll do what I can to make it a bit better."

Some might be inclined to think that people like Hal and Nick are just born as they are, or perhaps they are beneficiaries or victims of experiences in life that made them as they are. It could be a combination of the two actually, because our personalities are, in fact, shaped by both *nature and nurture*, as it's sometimes said. But there's something else. As adults, both Hal and Nick have the ability to look at a clear morning sky and see it with either joy or distain. They can either appreciate it or reject it. Both, however, *choose* what to think about it.

Readers may scoff at the claim that we choose how to feel about things. After all, how we feel is a reaction to what happens. We are human beings and we are programmed to react in certain ways. And I must admit that I agree with this basic premise to a large extent because our ability to react quickly to circumstances without having to waste time thinking about them has kept us alive as a species. I don't buy into the modern psycho-fluff peddled by some authors who want us to believe that we can live a life of utter bliss if we just make a conscious decision to react joyfully or patiently to everything that happens in our lives. Doesn't this sound wonderful? Who wouldn't want to buy into this? Well, it's both ridiculous and impractical.

You probably think I'm contradicting myself, don't you? Well, not entirely. I do believe that we are wired to react subconsciously and primitively to circumstances in our environment, which happens so fast that our initial reactions occur well before our conscious minds have a chance to start thinking about them.

Choice does play a significant role in our reactions, but only through the long-term engineering of our thinking habits. In the story above, Nick has conditioned himself over a long period of time to feel angry about what he sees as human negligence in the care of our planet. Hal, on the other hand, has conditioned himself to feel grateful for the beauty that exists in life. Both men looking at the same sky react to it very differently because for so long they've conditioned themselves in different ways. *It is the repetitive conditioning that is chosen, not our immediate reactions circumstances.* Our reactions in life draw their energy and consistency from our thinking habits. We are often unaware that we are choosing these habits, but we are. The reactions we experience in certain situations are simply logical outcomes caused by the thinking habits to which we've conditioned ourselves.

As a forensic scientist, you are in a career that has striking dualities and conflicting energies. On one hand, it is a profession of the utmost importance. It is intellectually stimulating and can bring a great sense of professional satisfaction. On the other hand, it is a profession that struggles with a chronic scarcity of resources. All the while it is charged with the responsibility of injecting high doses of science and logic into a system of justice plagued by adversarialism, political maneuvering, and an absence of cohesive leadership. Said another way, it can be both invigorating and demoralizing to serve as a forensic scientist. So, which do *you* choose?

As I said, it depends on how you condition yourself. As often as possible, bring your attention to things that happen in your professional life for which you are grateful. Remind yourself that you *get* to be a forensic scientist; you don't *have* to be one. You don't *have* to get up in the morning to work in a forensic science laboratory; you *get* to. This is what I mean by conditioned thinking. Try to imagine how the careers of two young forensic scientists will turn out when one makes a habit of being grateful for her work, her colleagues, and the opportunities her work brings, while the other focuses entirely on what's wrong, what she is unable to do, or what her career prevents her from doing? I, for one, can easily predict which forensic scientist is more likely to flourish in the years to come.

Of course, I am not suggesting that you should torture yourself by enduring professional hardships that are largely outside of your control. You should never tolerate chronic abuse, harassment, hostility, negligence, oppression, or any long-term behaviors unbecoming of a professional in a high-stakes, high-impact occupation. Nor should you for long tolerate feeling as if your professional growth and development have stalled. As a rule of thumb, your career and your work should never feel like a tour of duty, and you should never feel like you are having to endure mental and emotional pain as a condition of remaining gainfully employed. You are a professional, after all, and you should feel empowered, energized, and engaged.

By the same token, don't be too quick to judge others for any feelings of despair you may experience. You are quite capable of making *yourself* miserable by simply being impatient, overly demanding, or obsessive about things that frustrate you. Frustration is a part of life, and it is certainly a part of *professional* life. None of us are entitled to careers without frustration or careers free of the ups and downs that are part of the human experience.

I see myself as much more than an author. I see myself as your coach, and as your coach I have several hopes for you that will combine to deliver a career you can enjoy and feel rewarded by:

- Recognize the importance and value of forensic science
- Be grateful for the chance to work in such an interesting and impactful occupation
- Enjoy and appreciate the people you work with
- Develop and grow genuine friendships with as many work colleagues as possible
- Never stop being a student of forensic science; keep learning
- In your job, perform and behave in a way that makes you feel good about yourself and your profession
- Cut your laboratory managers and administrators some slack; they have very difficult jobs
- Use humor to deal with challenging interpersonal problems whenever possible
- Constantly check yourself
- Perform and behave in ways that make people appreciate your presence in the workplace
- Prioritize your team above yourself as often as possible

I know how much you want to enjoy your career, and you can if you are willing to make the choices necessary to earn that privilege. And as your career unfolds, the energy and enthusiasm you feel will make you more effective at dealing with or correcting the things that aren't so fun.

# 49

## Uplifting Your Coworkers

I'd like to have you do a little exercise, one that I like to have my clients do from time to time as a way to calibrate their thinking about their work and careers. It's simple – as you work at your desk or workbench, hopefully with other people around you, focus your awareness on the presence of your coworkers. As you do, think about the ways in which their own enjoyment of their work depends on *you*. In this moment, be mindful of how your choices and behaviors affect your colleagues – either positively or negatively. You only need to spend a few moments doing this, but really give it some effort. Then, as you keep your attention focused on your coworkers, I want you to think about the friends and family members of your coworkers and how they are impacted – positively or negatively – by how much or how little your coworkers enjoy their work. Now for the grand finale – think about how *your* choices and behaviors potentially affect all of these friends and family members – most of whom you probably have never met. Reflect for a moment on how important that makes you – that you have the potential to be so impactful to so many people.

Every day you come to work you have the opportunity to make the world a better place for so many people. No, your contributions may not splash the front page of the New York Times or win you a Nobel Peace Prize. Instead, the impact you have will be on the quality of life experienced by those within your influential reach. You won't necessarily see it happening, but you will *know* it's happening because you've made the people in your professional life a priority. Every time you have the opportunity to be kind, supportive, generous, friendly, encouraging, patient, and understanding, you will be changing the world.

As we near the end of this book, I challenge you – and I mean I *really* challenge you – to never waste the chance to uplift those with whom you work. Never stop thinking about the impact you have on other people, or how your words and behaviors cause people to either appreciate your presence or wish that you'd be subpoenaed to court on Mars. As you think about the impact you have on other people, you may not like what you realize. Perhaps you've been toxic. Maybe you've made no effort to be friendly or take an interest in others. Or, it could be that you are so mired in your own personal bitterness that you can't seem to summon an ounce of energy to give just one person the time of day. If that's you, I truly feel sorry for you – but only for a moment because I know for a fact that you can change simply by making the effort to change. Once you do, you can start feeling good about yourself and your career because you will have earned it.

For the majority of you that consistently make the forensic science laboratory a more fun and rewarding place to be, my hat's off to you. Keep doing it and never stop doing it because you are the engines that drive the entire profession. By making your laboratories a better place, you are making forensic science a better profession. With few exceptions, human beings are more effective when they enjoy what they are doing. So, when your words and behaviors are a source of that enjoyment, you have so much to be proud of and so much to feel good about. You've paid the price of admission to a career that really matters.

# 50

## Being a Forensic Science Ambassador

There's a special feeling that comes with knowing you represent an entire community of people whose credibility and perceived trustworthiness depend on you. Not only do you *practice* forensic science, you *represent* forensic science in everything you do and everything you say. I trust that when your professional stakeholders experience you and your expertise in action, their overall opinion of the profession is enhanced. As you go, so goes the profession of forensic science. The future and reputation of forensic science is on *your* shoulders and *your* shoulders alone. This is what it means to be an ambassador.

Among the many professional priorities I've adopted in my coaching and facilitation practices, I continue to make a significant effort to help forensic laboratory scientists understand the difference between a *profession* and a *specialty*. Forensic science is very segregated along discipline lines, and it is easy for forensic scientists to mistakenly attach their sense of professional identity to their specific disciplines. DNA analysts are separate and distinct from latent print examiners, for example, because the two areas of expertise share nothing in common, at least from a technical standpoint. DNA analysts care about DNA testing. Latent print examiners care about comparing latent prints. There's not much in common around which they can unite and collaborate. Or is there?

Yes, there is. Your profession is *not* your discipline. Your profession is forensic science. More specifically, if you work in a forensic science laboratory, your profession is the *forensic laboratory sciences*. Do not confuse your specialty with your profession, and please do not make the all-too-common mistake of becoming excessively loyal and attached to your discipline. If you do, you will blind yourself to the many other opportunities and responsibilities that will otherwise enrich your forensic science career. You will also erode your capacity to communicate and collaborate with forensic scientists in other disciplines, which is a great source of professional satisfaction, at least it was to me.

I think this is an important facet of being a forensic science ambassador – caring about all the disciplines and their interrelationships to each other. Over the course of your career, you will undoubtedly spend a lot of time and effort developing and refining your scientific expertise within a specific discipline. This is certainly a good thing. But don't ignore the many opportunities you will have to develop those areas of expertise that transcend your discipline, especially things dealing with the operation and administration of your laboratory and the criminal justice system it serves.

As you think about all the situations and opportunities we've explored in this book, and as you commit yourself to being the very best forensic scientist you can be, you can look at yourself in the mirror and see a *world-class* forensic science professional – an ambassador who proudly and consistently represents the profession with skill and honor. Not only is that a career you can feel good about, it is a career you can enjoy for many years to come!

# CONCLUSION

## You are likely to end up with the career you deserve

Time will tell if your forensic science career will confront you with all of the situations described in this book, but I can promise that you will be confronted by many of them. As I sit here in my office, I can reflect back on nearly 30 years of work in forensic science, recalling so many challenging situations and opportunities that collectively define the man and professional I've become. For me, I've encountered *every* situation described in this book and find great professional satisfaction in being able to help prepare you to encounter them as well.

Upon my admission that I've encountered all 50 of these situations, you may find it awkward that I would admit to #25, being tempted to lie or cheat. Well, this is not to suggest that I've ever felt tempted to steal something, lie on a report, or take a shortcut that I knew was in violation of our laboratory's policies and quality assurance standards. But I recall one situation, in particular, in which I had to go out of my way *not* to cheat.

It was August 28, 2000, which also happened to be my dad's 59th birthday. I had been promoted as the new laboratory director of the DuPage County Crime Laboratory in Wheaton, Illinois – about 30 miles due west of the Chicago Loop. Although the laboratory and its parent agency had some challenges that needed to be overcome, I was fortunate to have inherited the foundations of what would become a world-class staff that allowed us to create what became, in my opinion, a world-class forensic science laboratory. Serving a county of approximately a million people, we were highly respected, efficient, and productive. We practiced the most common forensic disciplines including firearm and toolmark identification, controlled substances testing, trace evidence testing, flammables and combustibles testing, latent print comparisons, DNA analysis, and others. The only common disciplines we didn't practice were forensic toxicology and questioned documents. In fact, our laboratory was sometimes used by the National Transportation Safety Board to test fuel samples in aircraft accidents. It was an honor to come to work every day to work in *that* laboratory with *that* staff. I miss them.

Not long after my promotion, I found myself spending an ever-increasing amount of time on issues related to the growth of our new DNA unit. CODIS was just coming on board and we wanted our laboratory to qualify for its installation. I couldn't help but feel empathy for our DNA technical leader, Doug, who was in the unenviable position of having to explain DNA principles to a laboratory director who was a firearm and toolmark examiner. This is not to say that I didn't grasp the things he was telling me. He was patient with me and very generous in helping to educate me. But our conversations exhausted valuable time during which he had to give me DNA tutorials before we ever got to the real issues at hand.

So, one day I called Doug into my office and asked him to have a seat. "Doug, so this is what I want to do," I began. "I want to spend a full week in the DNA unit. Other than dealing with any urgent matters requiring my attention, I'm going to take the week off from my director duties so I can spend it with you and the DNA staff. Whatever week we decide on, I'd like you to organize it so that I can experience and observe as much of what you do as possible. I want to be a DNA trainee for a week."

I could see Doug's face light up with eager anticipation as I made my request. And, as I'd hoped, he came through, making it one of the most memorable and useful weeks of my entire career. I was able to observe evidence being processed from the early serological stage to the final DNA confirmatory stage. To be candid, I don't think I ever spent a week in my career where I learned so much that I was able to apply in meeting my responsibilities as a forensic laboratory administrator. From that moment on, every conversation I had with Doug or another member of the DNA staff was efficient and engaging. I understood the process. I understood the language. When I was told, for example, of problems occurring with the thermocycler in post-amp, I understood what that meant and why it was problematic. For the remainder of my career as a forensic laboratory director, the week I spent with Doug and his team in our DNA unit dramatically improved the effectiveness of my leadership, not only in DuPage County but also during my tenure as the director of forensic science for the state of Michigan.

The reason I share this story with you is because it was tempting to cheat. I could have easily just continued the way we were going and be satisfied with subjecting Doug and myself to laborious conversations in which I was ill-equipped to provide the managerial supports and approvals that our DNA unit needed during its early years. After all, I was the director. I had the power and authority. It was up to Doug and his team to cope with me, right? – to cope with whatever limitations I brought to our conversations. But, again, that would have been *cheating*, and that's not what I'm about. The right thing to do, in my mind, was to strengthen my position in those conversations by understanding our DNA unit, its processes, and its people in such a way that I could collaborate with them more effectively.

One of the ironic things about being a professional is that our career effectiveness is perpetually limited by an innate tendency toward laziness. Human beings, as with all living creatures, survive by being able to live safely and comfortably while expending as little energy as possible. A rattle snake hiding under a rock near a busy sidewalk is something to be frightened of, but it doesn't want to bite anyone because it takes too much energy to do so. This is energy better spent on hunting for food, water, or shelter. As an executive coach, I confront *innate laziness* on a regular basis. As much as struggling clients like to think that factors beyond their control are causing whatever disappointments or frustrations they are feeling, more often than not they are allowing their innate laziness to impair their ability to influence the people and circumstances in their environment.

So, are we therefore doomed to be lazy? Thankfully not. The inhibitory power of innate laziness is overcome by *inspiration*. Inspiration is what drives people to exhaust their finite energy when it would be so much easier to just be safe and comfortable. In my interactions with my DNA unit so many years ago, my own innate laziness could have easily dominated my internal dialogue, dissuading me from investing the time and energy needed to educate myself and enhance the quality of the interpersonal connections I had with my DNA staff. Thankfully, I felt inspired

Admittedly, some people are more easily inspired than others, while some people have a stronger affinity for safety and comfort than others. In my opinion, the people we witness enjoying tremendous amounts of career success are those who are easily inspired. They recognize problems and possibilities and are motivated to engage them. They have a strong desire to self-actuate, which is to do meaningful things in this temporary life of uncertain duration. People who are inspired are the ones that make things happen.

Conversely, those we witness dutifully pushing through careers that are average or disappointing are those with a stronger sense of innate laziness. It takes much more inspiration for them to overcome their natural desire to take it easy. Interestingly, these struggling professionals often feel like they are working hard, because they actually are. It's much harder for them to put forth the kind of mental or physical effort that inspired people do. So, when you try to challenge the innately lazy to be more productive or engaged, they are often surprised and possibly offended by the suggestion that they are not contributing their fair share.

The truth of the matter is, however, that we *all* struggle to overcome the adverse consequences of innate laziness. You do and I do. More important, however, are the conditioned thinking habits we develop as the result of adhering to repeating patterns of decision-making. The more you seek to be inspired and act on that inspiration, the easier it will become and the more inspired you will be. The more you minimize your efforts and limit the amount of energy you expend, the less effective and less inspired you will be. This means that the career you end up with is likely the one you deserve because, like me, you enjoy so many opportunities to be inspired and have so many sources of knowledge and information from which to learn and build your professional expertise.

If I could add a 51st situation to this book, it would be your entire career. You are living out a situation right now. In fact, your very existence is a situation. So, what would you like to do with it? What are the possibilities? What's getting in your way? What choices can you make today that will give you a better tomorrow? Perhaps you've been making the right choices for a long time and you're enjoying the kind of career you always desired. Or maybe you've been making poor choices – or no choices at all – resulting in a feeling of being stuck or unable to break free of the professional resistance you are feeling. Either way, you always have the option to start making good choices today, starting right now. No matter what circumstances you face, hardships you've endured, or mistakes you've made in the past, you can hit the reset button in this very moment and start building a career and life that you can feel great about. It may take considerable time and effort, but these are what will give you the sense of satisfaction that comes from achieving *your* kind of success. People don't fail because they've made terminally catastrophic mistakes. They fail because they stop trying.

I'm going to close by repeating what I shared in the introduction of this book. Forensic science is a rewarding and invigorating occupation that holds as many secrets as it does promises. Whatever you do, be conscious about taking time to reflect on the gratitude that you have for being able to work in such a celebrated, respected field of endeavor. Millions of people around the world would love to have your job. Treat it with the respect it deserves as you treat yourself with the respect *you* deserve. And as you encounter some or all of the situations described in this book, and as you encounter any other situations that tax your mental and emotional energies, ask yourself this simple question:

*What would a world-class forensic scientist do in this situation?*

# APPENDIX

## Accelerated Professionalism Through Self-Analysis

I'd like to take this opportunity to facilitate the emergence of further insights unique to you and whatever personal and professional circumstances you may be encountering right now or in the future. As a professional coach, I'm trained and experienced in the art of asking questions in such a way that it forces people to see and understand themselves with more clarity. On the following pages, I am going to ask you 50 specific questions that I believe you must consider and answer if you are to maximize your success as a forensic science professional. For each question, I am going to leave space on the page for you to write out your answers and identify what priorities are implied or suggested in the answer you give. Then, at the bottom of the page, you are going to give yourself a score of 0 to 4, where 4 means that very clear and compelling priorities are implied or evident for you in the next year or two, while 0 means that no substantial priorities are implied or evident. On the final page of the appendix, I am going to have you add up your scores in a table you can use to help focus yourself on boosting your overall professionalism and self-awareness.

This exercise may take you days, weeks, or months to complete, so take as much time as you need. It is important that you think carefully about the questions and write out your answers because the act of writing them out has a powerful effect on boosting your sense of inspiration to make whatever changes you identify as needing prioritization. Like anything else, you will get out of this experience what you put into it!

1. Are you enjoying your career, or do you spend a lot of time wishing you were doing some*thing* else or doing it some*where* else?

___

What do you want to be different in the future?

___

What do you need to **start** doing or do **more** of?

___

What do you need to **stop** doing, or do **less** of?

___

4___Very High    3___High    2___Moderate    1___Low    0___Very Low

2. When your colleagues, coworkers, and managers think about you, what do you *want* them to think?

_____
_____
_____
_____
_____
_____
_____

What do you want to be different in the future?

_____
_____
_____
_____
_____
_____
_____
_____

What do you need to *start* doing or do *more* of?

_____
_____
_____
_____

What do you need to *stop* doing, or do *less* of?

_____
_____
_____
_____

4____Very High    3____High    2____Moderate    1____Low    0____Very Low

3. If your colleagues, coworkers, or managers gave me their honest opinions about you, what would they tell me?

_____
_____
_____
_____
_____
_____
_____

What do you want to be different in the future?

_____
_____
_____
_____
_____
_____
_____

What do you need to *start* doing or do *more* of?

_____
_____
_____
_____

What do you need to *stop* doing, or do *less* of?

_____
_____
_____
_____

4____Very High    3____High    2____Moderate    1____Low    0____Very Low

4. In what ways do you think or feel that *other* people are adversely impacting your sense of career/job satisfaction?

_____
_____
_____
_____
_____
_____

What do you want to be different in the future?

_____
_____
_____
_____
_____
_____
_____

What do you need to *start* doing or do *more* of?

_____
_____
_____
_____

What do you need to *stop* doing, or do *less* of?

_____
_____
_____
_____

4___Very High   3___High   2___Moderate   1___Low   0___Very Low

5. In what ways do you think or feel that *you* are adversely impacting your own sense of career/job satisfaction?

_____
_____
_____
_____
_____
_____
_____

What do you want to be different in the future?

_____
_____
_____
_____
_____
_____
_____
_____

What do you need to *start* doing or do *more* of?

_____
_____
_____
_____

What do you need to *stop* doing, or do *less* of?

_____
_____
_____
_____

4____Very High    3____High    2____Moderate    1____Low    0____Very Low

6. What do you like most about the profession of forensic science? What causes you to feel like you are in the right career?

_____
_____
_____
_____
_____
_____
_____

What do you want to be different in the future?

_____
_____
_____
_____
_____
_____
_____

What do you need to *start* doing or do *more* of?

_____
_____
_____
_____

What do you need to *stop* doing, or do *less* of?

_____
_____
_____
_____

4___Very High     3___High     2___Moderate     1___Low     0___Very Low

7. What do you like most about your current job location, including the facilities, the city, and geographical region in which you work and live?

_____
_____
_____
_____
_____
_____
_____

What do you want to be different in the future?

_____
_____
_____
_____
_____
_____
_____
_____

What do you need to *start* doing or do *more* of?

_____
_____
_____
_____

What do you need to *stop* doing, or do *less* of?

_____
_____
_____
_____

4____Very High    3____High    2____Moderate    1____Low    0____Very Low

8. What do you like most about the work you do and the responsibilities you currently have?

_____
_____
_____
_____
_____
_____
_____

What do you want to be different in the future?

_____
_____
_____
_____
_____
_____
_____

What do you need to *start* doing or do *more* of?

_____
_____
_____
_____

What do you need to *stop* doing, or do *less* of?

_____
_____
_____
_____

4____Very High    3____High    2____Moderate    1____Low    0____Very Low

9. Do you take an interest in the people with whom you work? Do you engage them in conversation or ask about things of interest to them?

_____
_____
_____
_____
_____
_____
_____

What do you want to be different in the future?

_____
_____
_____
_____
_____
_____
_____

What do you need to *start* doing or do *more* of?

_____
_____
_____
_____

What do you need to *stop* doing, or do *less* of?

_____
_____
_____
_____

4____Very High   3____High   2____Moderate   1____Low   0____Very Low

10. How would you describe the impact you have on your immediate work environment and the people in it?

___

What do you want to be different in the future?

___

What do you need to *start* doing or do *more* of?

___

What do you need to *stop* doing, or do *less* of?

___

4___Very High    3___High    2___Moderate    1___Low    0___Very Low

11. In what ways does *innate laziness* (as explained in the conclusion of this book) create problems for you and your professional performance?

_____
_____
_____
_____
_____
_____
_____

What do you want to be different in the future?

_____
_____
_____
_____
_____
_____
_____
_____

What do you need to *start* doing or do *more* of?

_____
_____
_____
_____

What do you need to *stop* doing, or do *less* of?

_____
_____
_____
_____

4___Very High    3___High    2___Moderate    1___Low    0___Very Low

12. In what ways does the *innate laziness* of others create problems for you and your professional performance?

What do you want to be different in the future?

What do you need to **start** doing or do **more** of?

What do you need to **stop** doing, or do **less** of?

4____Very High    3____High    2____Moderate    1____Low    0____Very Low

13. Are there people at work with whom you enjoy meaningful friendships? Who are they? What about them do you appreciate?

___

What do you want to be different in the future?

___

What do you need to *start* doing or do *more* of?

___

What do you need to *stop* doing, or do *less* of?

___

4____Very High    3____High    2____Moderate    1____Low    0____Very Low

14. Does your current job and its responsibilities allow you to learn new things and apply them in the execution of meaningful work?

_____
_____
_____
_____
_____
_____
_____

What do you want to be different in the future?

_____
_____
_____
_____
_____
_____
_____
_____

What do you need to *start* doing or do *more* of?

_____
_____
_____
_____

What do you need to *stop* doing, or do *less* of?

_____
_____
_____
_____

4____Very High     3____High     2____Moderate     1____Low     0____Very Low

15. Are you a team player? Do your professional performance and behaviors bring the best out of the people with whom you work?

_____
_____
_____
_____
_____
_____
_____

What do you want to be different in the future?

_____
_____
_____
_____
_____
_____
_____

What do you need to *start* doing or do *more* of?

_____
_____
_____
_____

What do you need to *stop* doing, or do *less* of?

_____
_____
_____
_____

4____Very High    3____High    2____Moderate    1____Low    0____Very Low

16. What are the sources or causes of chronic stress for you at work? What makes your job most challenging?

_____
_____
_____
_____
_____
_____
_____

What do you want to be different in the future?

_____
_____
_____
_____
_____
_____
_____
_____

What do you need to *start* doing or do *more* of?

_____
_____
_____
_____

What do you need to *stop* doing, or do *less* of?

_____
_____
_____
_____

4____Very High    3____High    2____Moderate    1____Low    0____Very Low

17. When you have conversations with people, how much talking do you do? How much listening do you do? Is there a balance?

_____
_____
_____
_____
_____
_____
_____
_____

What do you want to be different in the future?

_____
_____
_____
_____
_____
_____
_____
_____

What do you need to *start* doing or do *more* of?

_____
_____
_____
_____

What do you need to *stop* doing, or do *less* of?

_____
_____
_____
_____

4____Very High    3____High    2____Moderate    1____Low    0____Very Low

18. Do you understand what is expected of you in your current job, or do you feel confused in any way? Is there a lack of clarity?

_____
_____
_____
_____
_____

What do you want to be different in the future?

_____
_____
_____
_____
_____

What do you need to *start* doing or do *more* of?

_____
_____
_____

What do you need to *stop* doing, or do *less* of?

_____
_____
_____

4____Very High    3____High    2____Moderate    1____Low    0____Very Low

19. Do you have the equipment and supplies needed to do your job reasonably well?

_____
_____
_____
_____
_____
_____
_____
_____

What do you want to be different in the future?

_____
_____
_____
_____
_____
_____
_____
_____

What do you need to *start* doing or do *more* of?

_____
_____
_____
_____

What do you need to *stop* doing, or do *less* of?

_____
_____
_____
_____

**4**___Very High    **3**___High    **2**___Moderate    **1**___Low    **0**___Very Low

20. Are you good at what you do? Has your training, education, and experience allowed you to be competent in your work?

What do you want to be different in the future?

What do you need to *start* doing or do *more* of?

What do you need to *stop* doing, or do *less* of?

4____Very High    3____High    2____Moderate    1____Low    0____Very Low

21. Does your supervisor genuinely care about you as a person? Does he or she take an interest in both your work and your well-being?

_____
_____
_____
_____
_____
_____
_____

What do you want to be different in the future?

_____
_____
_____
_____
_____
_____
_____

What do you need to *start* doing or do *more* of?

_____
_____
_____
_____

What do you need to *stop* doing, or do *less* of?

_____
_____
_____
_____

4____Very High     3____High     2____Moderate     1____Low     0____Very Low

22. In the last year, has anyone mentored or coached you in an effective way such that it gave you valuable insights? What were they?

_____
_____
_____
_____
_____
_____
_____

What do you want to be different in the future?

_____
_____
_____
_____
_____
_____
_____

What do you need to *start* doing or do *more* of?

_____
_____
_____
_____

What do you need to *stop* doing, or do *less* of?

_____
_____
_____
_____

4___Very High    3___High    2___Moderate    1___Low    0___Very Low

23. Is your total rewards (compensation + benefits + job value) reasonably fair and equitable?

_____
_____
_____
_____
_____
_____
_____

What do you want to be different in the future?

_____
_____
_____
_____
_____
_____
_____

What do you need to *start* doing or do *more* of?

_____
_____
_____
_____

What do you need to *stop* doing, or do *less* of?

_____
_____
_____
_____

4____Very High    3____High    2____Moderate    1____Low    0____Very Low

24. How often do you have days when you really *love* your job? What causes you to feel that way?

What do you want to be different in the future?

What do you need to *start* doing or do **more** of?

What do you need to *stop* doing, or do **less** of?

4____Very High    3____High    2____Moderate    1____Low    0____Very Low

25. How often do you have days when you really *dislike* your job? What causes you to feel that way?

_____
_____
_____
_____
_____
_____
_____

What do you want to be different in the future?

_____
_____
_____
_____
_____
_____
_____

What do you need to *start* doing or do *more* of?

_____
_____
_____
_____

What do you need to *stop* doing, or do *less* of?

_____
_____
_____
_____

4____Very High    3____High    2____Moderate    1____Low    0____Very Low

26. How often do you offend or irritate people with your words and behaviors? Provide some examples if you can?

_____
_____
_____
_____
_____
_____

What do you want to be different in the future?

_____
_____
_____
_____
_____
_____
_____

What do you need to *start* doing or do *more* of?

_____
_____
_____
_____

What do you need to *stop* doing, or do *less* of?

_____
_____
_____
_____

4____Very High    3____High    2____Moderate    1____Low    0____Very Low

27. How often do you encourage people or express thoughts that make them feel valued and appreciated?

_____
_____
_____
_____
_____
_____
_____

What do you want to be different in the future?

_____
_____
_____
_____
_____
_____
_____
_____

What do you need to *start* doing or do *more* of?

_____
_____
_____
_____

What do you need to *stop* doing, or do *less* of?

_____
_____
_____
_____

4___Very High   3___High   2___Moderate   1___Low   0___Very Low

28. Are you willing and able to engage in conflict, disagreements, or arguments with people at work without feeling panicked or paralyzed?

_____
_____
_____
_____
_____
_____

What do you want to be different in the future?

_____
_____
_____
_____
_____
_____
_____

What do you need to *start* doing or do *more* of?

_____
_____
_____

What do you need to *stop* doing, or do *less* of?

_____
_____
_____
_____

4____Very High     3____High     2____Moderate     1____Low     0____Very Low

29. Are you flexible and adaptable when change occurs? Do you help with the transition or do you create resistance?

_____
_____
_____
_____
_____
_____
_____
_____

What do you want to be different in the future?

_____
_____
_____
_____
_____
_____
_____
_____

What do you need to *start* doing or do *more* of?

_____
_____
_____
_____

What do you need to *stop* doing, or do *less* of?

_____
_____
_____
_____

4____Very High    3____High    2____Moderate    1____Low    0____Very Low

30. Are you chronically frustrated with management and judgmental of its intentions, or are you supportive, patient, and understanding?

What do you want to be different in the future?

What do you need to *start* doing or do *more* of?

What do you need to *stop* doing, or do *less* of?

4___Very High    3___High    2___Moderate    1___Low    0___Very Low

31. Do you consider yourself a dominant personality or submissive personality? How does this impact your professional life?

_____
_____
_____
_____
_____
_____
_____

What do you want to be different in the future?

_____
_____
_____
_____
_____
_____
_____
_____

What do you need to *start* doing or do *more* of?

_____
_____
_____
_____
_____

What do you need to *stop* doing, or do *less* of?

_____
_____
_____
_____

4____Very High    3____High    2____Moderate    1____Low    0____Very Low

32. How often do you smile and laugh with people at work? Do you make a conscious effort to smile when greeting colleagues?

_____
_____
_____
_____
_____
_____

What do you want to be different in the future?

_____
_____
_____
_____
_____
_____
_____
_____

What do you need to *start* doing or do *more* of?

_____
_____
_____
_____

What do you need to *stop* doing, or do *less* of?

_____
_____
_____
_____

4___Very High   3___High   2___Moderate   1___Low   0___Very Low

33. In meetings or conversations, do you make a point of asking good questions to help spark discussion and the sharing of ideas?

_____
_____
_____
_____
_____
_____
_____

What do you want to be different in the future?

_____
_____
_____
_____
_____
_____
_____

What do you need to *start* doing or do *more* of?

_____
_____
_____
_____

What do you need to *stop* doing, or do *less* of?

_____
_____
_____
_____

4___Very High   3___High   2___Moderate   1___Low   0___Very Low

34. In meetings or conversations, are you preoccupied by what you want to say, or do you listen carefully to what others are sharing?

What do you want to be different in the future?

What do you need to *start* doing or do *more* of?

What do you need to *stop* doing, or do *less* of?

4___Very High    3___High    2___Moderate    1___Low    0___Very Low

35. Do you consider yourself a "friend and colleague to all" or do you operate in small cliques or groups that exclude or marginalize others?

_____
_____
_____
_____
_____
_____
_____

What do you want to be different in the future?

_____
_____
_____
_____
_____
_____
_____

What do you need to *start* doing or do *more* of?

_____
_____
_____
_____

What do you need to *stop* doing, or do *less* of?

_____
_____
_____
_____

4____Very High    3____High    2____Moderate    1____Low    0____Very Low

36. At work, how often do you behave in a way that a reasonable person would describe as kind, generous, and thoughtful?

_____
_____
_____
_____
_____
_____

What do you want to be different in the future?

_____
_____
_____
_____
_____
_____
_____

What do you need to *start* doing or do *more* of?

_____
_____
_____

What do you need to *stop* doing, or do *less* of?

_____
_____
_____
_____

4____Very High    3____High    2____Moderate    1____Low    0____Very Low

37. How easy is it for you to admit openly that you made a mistake, that you are sorry, or that there's something you aren't very good at?

_____
_____
_____
_____
_____
_____

What do you want to be different in the future?

_____
_____
_____
_____
_____
_____
_____
_____

What do you need to *start* doing or do *more* of?

_____
_____
_____
_____

What do you need to *stop* doing, or do *less* of?

_____
_____
_____
_____

4____Very High    3____High    2____Moderate    1____Low    0____Very Low

38. Are you generally willing to extend trust to others even though it may expose you to some risk – or are you guarded and defensive?

_____
_____
_____
_____
_____
_____
_____
_____

What do you want to be different in the future?

_____
_____
_____
_____
_____
_____
_____
_____

What do you need to *start* doing or do *more* of?

_____
_____
_____
_____

What do you need to *stop* doing, or do *less* of?

_____
_____
_____
_____

4____Very High     3____High     2____Moderate     1____Low     0____Very Low

39. Are you clear with people how you feel about things or where you stand on issues, or do you play politics and manipulate conversations?

_____
_____
_____
_____
_____
_____
_____

What do you want to be different in the future?

_____
_____
_____
_____
_____
_____
_____

What do you need to *start* doing or do *more* of?

_____
_____
_____
_____

What do you need to *stop* doing, or do *less* of?

_____
_____
_____
_____

4____Very High    3____High    2____Moderate    1____Low    0____Very Low

40. Do you treat *every* person at work with courtesy, dignity, and respect regardless of their rank, experience, or stature?

What do you want to be different in the future?

What do you need to *start* doing or do *more* of?

What do you need to *stop* doing, or do *less* of?

4____Very High    3____High    2____Moderate    1____Low    0____Very Low

41. Do you make your intentions known to others? Do your coworkers know and understand what your true goals and ambitions are?

_____
_____
_____
_____
_____
_____
_____

What do you want to be different in the future?

_____
_____
_____
_____
_____
_____
_____

What do you need to *start* doing or do *more* of?

_____
_____
_____
_____

What do you need to *stop* doing, or do *less* of?

_____
_____
_____
_____

4____Very High    3____High    2____Moderate    1____Low    0____Very Low

42. When you've done something to offend or hurt someone else, do you atone for your actions, apologize, and attempt to make it right?

_____
_____
_____
_____
_____
_____

What do you want to be different in the future?

_____
_____
_____
_____
_____
_____

What do you need to *start* doing or do *more* of?

_____
_____
_____

What do you need to *stop* doing, or do *less* of?

_____
_____
_____

4____Very High    3____High    2____Moderate    1____Low    0____Very Low

43. When was the last time you spoke highly about a coworker or manager behind her or his back? Is this something you do often?

_____
_____
_____
_____
_____
_____
_____

What do you want to be different in the future?

_____
_____
_____
_____
_____
_____
_____
_____

What do you need to *start* doing or do *more* of?

_____
_____
_____
_____

What do you need to *stop* doing, or do *less* of?

_____
_____
_____
_____

4____Very High     3____High     2____Moderate     1____Low     0____Very Low

44. Are you a person that gets things done, makes things happen, and can be trusted to execute effectively on work and projects?

_____
_____
_____
_____
_____
_____
_____

What do you want to be different in the future?

_____
_____
_____
_____
_____
_____
_____
_____
_____

What do you need to *start* doing or do *more* of?

_____
_____
_____
_____

What do you need to *stop* doing, or do *less* of?

_____
_____
_____
_____

4____Very High    3____High    2____Moderate    1____Low    0____Very Low

45. Do you tackle issues and problems head on? When something isn't right or needs attention, do you take the initiative to address it?

_____
_____
_____
_____
_____
_____
_____

What do you want to be different in the future?

_____
_____
_____
_____
_____
_____
_____

What do you need to *start* doing or do *more* of?

_____
_____
_____
_____

What do you need to *stop* doing, or do *less* of?

_____
_____
_____
_____

4____Very High     3____High     2____Moderate     1____Low     0____Very Low

46. Do you hold yourself accountable for your behaviors and performance or do you try to get away with things?

_____
_____
_____
_____
_____
_____

What do you want to be different in the future?

_____
_____
_____
_____
_____
_____

What do you need to *start* doing or do *more* of?

_____
_____
_____
_____

What do you need to *stop* doing, or do *less* of?

_____
_____
_____
_____

4____Very High    3____High    2____Moderate    1____Low    0____Very Low

47. Do you keep your promises and commitments? When you say you are going to do something, do you do it? Do you do it promptly?

_____
_____
_____
_____
_____
_____
_____
_____

What do you want to be different in the future?

_____
_____
_____
_____
_____
_____
_____
_____

What do you need to *start* doing or do *more* of?

_____
_____
_____
_____

What do you need to *stop* doing, or do *less* of?

_____
_____
_____
_____

4____Very High    3____High    2____Moderate    1____Low    0____Very Low

48. Do you have a core set of values or principles that guide your conduct and influence how you make professional decisions?

_____
_____
_____
_____
_____
_____

What do you want to be different in the future?

_____
_____
_____
_____
_____
_____
_____

What do you need to *start* doing or do *more* of?

_____
_____
_____

What do you need to *stop* doing, or do *less* of?

_____
_____
_____
_____

4____Very High     3____High     2____Moderate     1____Low     0____Very Low

49. How would it make you feel if I told you that you are going to end up having the life and career you deserve? Is that good or bad?

_____
_____
_____
_____
_____
_____
_____
_____

What do you want to be different in the future?

_____
_____
_____
_____
_____
_____
_____
_____

What do you need to *start* doing or do *more* of?

_____
_____
_____
_____

What do you need to *stop* doing, or do *less* of?

_____
_____
_____
_____

4___Very High    3___High    2___Moderate    1___Low    0___Very Low

50. What are your true intentions? How do your true intentions manifest themselves in how you speak, behave, and perform?

_____
_____
_____
_____
_____
_____

What do you want to be different in the future?

_____
_____
_____
_____
_____
_____
_____
_____

What do you need to *start* doing or do *more* of?

_____
_____
_____

What do you need to *stop* doing, or do *less* of?

_____
_____
_____
_____

4___Very High    3___High    2___Moderate    1___Low    0___Very Low

**Professional Priorities**
In the spaces below, write the priority score for each question:

| | | | |
|---|---|---|---|
| 1 _____ | 21 _____ | 41 _____ | **Total Score:** |
| 2 _____ | 22 _____ | 42 _____ | _____/200 |
| 3 _____ | 23 _____ | 43 _____ | **Average Score:** |
| 4 _____ | 24 _____ | 44 _____ | _____/4 |
| 5 _____ | 25 _____ | 45 _____ | **Number of 4s:** |
| 6 _____ | 26 _____ | 46 _____ | _____/50 |
| 7 _____ | 27 _____ | 47 _____ | **Number of 3s/2s:** |
| 8 _____ | 28 _____ | 48 _____ | _____/50 |
| 9 _____ | 29 _____ | 49 _____ | **Number of 1s/0s:** |
| 10 _____ | 30 _____ | 50 _____ | _____/50 |

11 _____      31 _____

12 _____      32 _____      **Making Positive Change**
                            After you have entered your scores for
13 _____      33 _____      each question, circle the three that
                            represent your top priorities in the
14 _____      34 _____      coming 2 to 3 years – those that are
                            most likely to have the most
15 _____      35 _____      significant positive impact on your
                            work, your career, and your job
16 _____      36 _____      performance. Then:

17 _____      37 _____      1. Create a personal plan

18 _____      38 _____      2. Hold yourself accountable

                            3. Create new thinking habits
19 _____      39 _____
                            4. Ask for help when you need it
20 _____      40 _____
                            5. Ask others to check you

# About the Author

John Collins is an executive coach, leadership facilitator, and forensic organizational clinician. He specializes in helping people, teams, and organizations having a mission of high public consequence. He started his private practice in 2013 after retiring his award-winning, 20-year career in forensic science, having served as the director of forensic science for the state of Michigan and authoring two pioneering textbooks on forensic science leadership and public policy. As a facilitator, John's range of experience is unmatched, having facilitated corporate strategic planning sessions, as well as highly sensitive domestic and international meetings on behalf of the United States Government. John's career highlights include his part in the forensic investigation of the Atlanta serial bombings, which included the bombing of the 1996 Olympics in Atlanta (for which he received a commendation from the Department of the Treasury), as well as his 2013 participation in a historic meeting with Attorney General Eric Holder and other experts to discuss solutions to gun crime following the Sandy Hook Elementary School shooting. In his practice, John utilizes a unique method that combines principles of executive coaching and leadership education with forensic analytical methods that quickly and accurately identify opportunities for his clients to improve their professional effectiveness. John has a master's degree in Organizational Management and is formally certified as a senior HR professional by the Society for Human Resource Management (SHRM). In 2012, John was trained as a professional coach by the College of Executive Coaching. He lives and works near Detroit. To learn more about John and his practice, please visit **criticalvictories.com**.